YOUR LIFE IS A MOVIE

YOUR LIFE IS A MOVIE

Alternative Visions of Film, Media, and Culture:
The Best of SolPix, 2002-2005

Edited by Don Thompson and Nicholas Rombes

)•)

Del Sol Press • Washington, DC

To enlightenment, in all its guises...

CONTENTS

Preface

PREFACE

by Don Thompson
and Nicholas Rombes

A few years ago, in 1999, I mentioned to director Rob Nilsson at a retrospective of his films at the Mill Valley Film Festival that I thought we needed the American equivalent of a new *Cahiers Du Cinéma,* the influential
French film publication co-founded by André Bazin in the 1950's, whose
early essayists included the legendary filmmakers Francois Truffault and
Jean-Luc Godard, among others. My sense, dating back to my days at UCLA
film school, was that media criticism had become too obtuse and specialized, wrapped in the cryptic language of Semiotics, Freud, and The
Frankfurt School. While I found myself fascinated in film school by an array
of philosophers, whether that be of Foucault or Sartre or Barthes, I also
found myself struggling with how any of these ideas would ever reach out to
a wider audience outside of academia. I longed for an accessible criticism,
one that was not afraid of current politics or the culture wars, or of challenging its readership to think about media issues in a new way. And yet this
"new criticism" would not be associated in any way shape or form to the
least common denominator influence of access and money which seems to
color US mainstream film critics and media pundits who find themselves
wrapped up in the megalithic PR machine that reflects the so called "media
market" in this country.

While I shelved these concerns and passions for many years as I pursued
other interests, they resurfaced again with the webzine and the power of
the Internet to reach so many instantly, all available through the "pull" of
web browsers and search engines. Due to the sheer luck of timing and
events, it seemed SolPix's exploration of media themes was quite *apropos*
to the early 2000's, which saw after 9/11 much of the media consolidating
ever more tightly into a truly corporate mindset that squeezed out political
diversity and, specifically, progressive ideas.

Truth be told, such a "corporate media" doesn't exist anymore in this country as a ubiquitous, monolithic voice (as Nick Rombes and Todd Gitlin will

point out later). And yet for many people in this country corporate media is a monolithic voice, and does constitute their main portal to the world. And this should concern us. In my view, this corporate or traditional media has become more conservative, cynical, risk-averse and compromised (all in the name of profits), even as the Internet blooms with diverse and independent voices. The rise of the Internet was, in fact, one of the excuses that media providers used to try to push through legislation that would expand caps on how much a particular company could own (in terms of market share) in the U.S., and also remove the barriers that kept broadcasters from owning newspapers. Both moves were fortunately defeated (one of the great success stories of cooperation from both sides of the political spectrum). My point is that we have two parallel trends: one that sees an ever more monolithic "corporate media" (be that broadcasters or film studios/distributors) that is vertically integrated and part of a conglomerate, and the other toward fragmentation of the media market through the Internet, satellite and cable. Trends in both "corporate" and "nontraditional" media, on analysis, are certainly related and in reaction to one another—but there's no time for that in this short preface. But it is the ever more conservative corporate media that by far has the ear of most Americans.

Another concern voiced through SolPix essays has been the wane of humanism in media. Now by humanism I mean, in general, a stance that defines human beings as inherently good, sees hatred and/or ignorance and psychological and economic factors as the primary drivers of "evil acts"—that "good and evil" debates miss the true underpinnings of our social problems, be they crime or drugs or the war on terror. The death of humanism can also be seen in the so-called "independent" film in the U.S. (that is, those films that get wide distribution and are still dubbed "independent"), which are more clever adult cartoons than anything hinting at the humanistic. Increasingly, the expression of humanism in film comes from outside the U.S., from documentary filmmakers such as Kayoko Mitsumatsu, or from within the U.S. by fiercely independent directors such as Rob Nilsson (interviews of both Mitsumatsu and Nilsson are included in this anthology). Fortunately, some recent U.S. mainstream and independent films, both documentary and narrative, seem to be bucking this trend; whether this bodes a renaissance for U.S.-made humanistic films remains to be seen. Certainly 2005 proved to be a banner year for the socially- and politically-relevant film, with directors such as George Clooney (*Good Night and Good Luck*), Paul Haggis (*Crash*) and Stephen Gaghan (*Syriana*) leading the way.

Preface

It is through the diminishment of humanism that the more conservative elements of this country have thus far successfully framed the cultural debate,
and once framed it becomes a *fait accompli* that they should control the
game. Both the "liberal" and "conservative" media often talk about "good
and evil" as if it was a given, some kind of reality that is etched in our
genes and only briefly challenged by "moral relativism" of the much-
abhorred postmodernism of the 1960's. But moral relativism was never the
agenda of humanism in my mind—for humanism, or moreover, a spiritual or
even Christian humanism—can be profoundly and consistently moral at its
core. Ray Carney and Eric Alterman are excellent examples of that "moral
yet critical" stance. (In fact, our founding fathers, especially Thomas
Jefferson, are pretty good examples too!) The challenge is, of course, not
to become moralistic, but rather to nurture a consistent moral core that is
at the same time rational and critical in its mindset and fundamentally
humanistic, compassionate and tolerant in its outlook. This kind of renewed
moral stance among progressives is, I believe, what attracted tens of thousands of unique readers to SolPix. And we weren't alone.

The publication of SolPix coincided with the rise (or resurrection in some
cases) of Amy Goodman, Noam Chomsky, Gore Vidal, Eric Alterman, Todd
Gitlin, Air America and others in a resurgence of the progressive left to a
more mainstream status, a resurgence that provided us with confident voices of balance during the difficult times post 9/11. SolPix found itself as a
vehicle, in many respects, of that resurgence.

I'd like to thank the many writers who have contributed to SolPix over the
last five years, some which have stayed with us, others who have moved on.
Writers such as Elizabeth Block, Kimberly Nichols, Mike Shen—all who
worked with us in the early days—and our regulars: Nick Rombes, Timothy
Dugdale, Patricia Ducey and T.B. ("Tom") Meek. Add to those our contributing writers and interviews from the likes of Todd Gitlin, Ray Carney, Eric
Alterman, Rob Nilsson and others, and we found some very powerful and
interesting voices being expressed through SolPix. While I have not agreed
with everything everybody has written for SolPix, I've always felt we reflect-
ed a wide array of views and opinions, and certainly been a good forum for
debate.

I'd especially like to thank Nick Rombes for co-editing this anthology. Nick
has always kept me on my toes, made me think, and provided a much needed and professional perspective.

And last but not least we have to thank the WebDelSol Editor-in-Chief, Michael Neff, web publishing visionary and courageous pioneer of the new web-based literary movement. Without Mike's support and unwavering trust, SolPix would have never been.

We at SolPix have attempted to hold a critical light to media trends, to the extent that we can. That attempt has been in a spirit of generosity—a gift to our readers because we fundamentally care enough about culture to write about it passionately and be a concerned voice that critiques our worst vices. While certainly we aren't the only voice, we have tried to be a consistent and courageous one that isn't afraid of the tough issues and big ideas: that is, the issues and ideas that mainstream media considers taboo as they put forward their own brand of self-defined relevance. And what is that relevance? Bad culture trumped up as good, mediocrity lifted to the spotlight even as excellence is drowned out, human values eclipsed by the excesses of an absolutist attitude of "good and evil" in all spheres, the aggressive and loud enemies of humanism and the human spirit—enemies who apparently believe that enlightened, empowered and self-aware individuals do not make for good business or manageable politics.

We hope that we have had some success in our efforts, and that you will continue supporting us with your readership, which is much valued.

Don Thompson
Washington DC, May 2006

One of the happy consequences of the Internet is its surprises. Because it grows and changes every day—every minute—there's no telling what sort of kindred spirits you might bump into surfing. I first came across SolPix in 2003 by sheer accident. I was hooked. Here, under the steady editorial guidance of Don Thompson, was writing that wasn't afraid to make Big Connections between movies and culture and that wasn't hobbled by the predictable likes and dislikes. Its mix of essays, polemics, interviews, and reviews somehow reminded me of the best parts of Pauline Kael and Lester Bangs, who wrote a sort of public theory, a populist theory that recognized that adopted a respectful hostility towards readers.

Our confessionalist era of reality TV, blogs, and other media forums which elevate the most mundane to the level of public pronouncement operates in a sort of double logic. On the one hand, it's easy to see that new technologies don't always result in vital new forms of expression. As Ray Carney asks in his interview in this anthology, "Did film criticism suddenly improve because of the invention of the VCR and DVD?" Probably not. But perhaps the proper question should be, "Do we still need film criticism in an era when film already critiques itself?" Let's face it, at some point film theory became outstripped in terms of aesthetic power by the very films it was critiquing. What made writers like Max Horkheimer, Theodor Adorno, Roland Barthes, Pauline Kael, Susan Sontag, Marshall McLuhan, Lester Bangs and others so vital was the fact that more often than not their writing constituted a stance, an attitude. Their writing—cranky, full of detours, idiosyncratic—was as shimmering and alive as many of the films, media, and music they wrote about.

In the institutionalization of film and media studies as an academic specialty in the 1960s, most of what made media criticism great was drained away. Academic film studies has always had a sort of inferiority complex, worried that it wasn't as rigorous, pure, or technical enough to gain legitimacy with the social sciences crowd. After all, film studies is a notoriously hybrid discipline. The effort of film and media studies folks to prove their worth and value to the tired administrators to whom they answer has unfortunately killed off the element of risk-taking obsolescence that is required for genuinely fierce and beautiful critique. The best writing about film has rarely been purely academic; rather its writers often hung around the edges of academia, lured by its promise of pure theory, but wary of its soul-killing bureaucracy and terminal lack of humor. It's the rare academic—like Ray Carney or Robert Ray—who manages to continue writing with a sense of surprise and danger from within the halls of academe.

In fact, it is this very stance—the stance of the outsider—that characterizes the best of what has appeared in SolPix, and which is collected in these pages. The strongest thread that links these essays, polemics, and interviews together is their shared belief that dangerous movies deserve to be written about dangerously. At its best, the writing in this anthology throws off sparks that illuminate the contours of that danger.

The position today is not that movies are bad or any worse than they were in the past, but rather that, in our cynicism and exhaustion, we risk missing the beauty and strangeness of everyday cinema. If in the 1960s, critics like Pauline Kael and Susan Sontag—in very different ways—defended "trash" or "pop culture" in the face of elitist high art, then the near-total triumph and ubiquity today of pop culture perhaps tempts us to lament the loss of "serious" or pure "art" films. But this is sheer nostalgia for a golden age that never existed. In today's cinema, the distinction between experimental and mainstream is shattered. Films like *The Blair Witch Project, Eternal Sunshine of the Spotless Mind, Memento, Last Days, The Celebration, Time Code*, and others are formalist experiments embedded in traditional genre modes.

While some of the essays here declaim against a corporate vision that undermines both moviemaking and the industry of film reviewing, it's also true that new technologies have made it possible to bypass such control mechanisms. One need only look to the numerous movie-oriented blogs, vlogs, and internet journals, where you can find writing that is alive and not bound by the editorial and advertising pressures of traditional print publications. This new digital public sphere is democratic; what's remarkable is not how amateurish or error-ridden it is, but rather how insightful and well-written much of it is. Clicking from a well-written amateur blog to an on-line movie review by one of our better-known movie critics, you feel suddenly free from the tyranny of the opinions of a Few over the Many. The description of *Donnie Darko* by authors you've never heard of at Wikedpedia.com—much like the user comments on the Internet Movie Database—are a form of resurrected New Criticism. Who could have predicted that the New Critical hallmark of close reading, of reading for plot, of hermeneutics, would not only persist but thrive in our era of personality-obsessed confessionalism?

The danger today is not that there is not enough good and vivid writing about film, but that there is too much of it. Did I say yet that I think this is a good thing? I do. And yet who can deny that the sheer abundance of this writing is exhausting. Online blogs and film journals that contain links to numerous other blogs and film journals make it easier to be amazed, and also more unlikely. In the old days of print, you could at least fool yourself into thinking that you had read the last and definitive word on a subject. No more. The trick has been exposed. The magician was a fraud. The stage has been stormed and all his secrets have been revealed. The rabbit came out of the hat and did not return. The old authorities—professors, critics, various experts—are subject to the same thumbs up, thumbs down as movies themselves. One of the happy consequences of this shake-up is that it has thrown together folks who have discovered that, all along, they shared similar passions. Thus, in this anthology we have filmmakers, professors, film critics, screenplay and fiction writers and others mixing it up.

Earlier I asked if we still needed film criticism in the era of self-theorizing media. The answer is yes, as long as the writing lives up to the humor, menace, and disequilibrium that the best movies promise. If writing has always offered one path of escape from the tyranny of the image, it is our hope that this anthology reminds you that this tyranny—sometimes, and when you least expect it—can be a beautiful thing.

Nick Rombes
Ann Arbor, MI, April 2006

AN INTERVIEW WITH RAY CARNEY

Warning: life altering, illusion shattering material enclosed

by Shelley Friedman

Editor's Note: We not only decided to publish the lightly edited text of Shelley Friedman's interview with Ray Carney, which originally appeared on the SolPix website as a shortened version, but to allow Friedman and Carney to add to it and bring it up-to-date in a few places. The interview covers a vast range of issues and ideas that we feel are important to our readers. Since the original version appeared in the first issue of SolPix, we place it first in this anthology, ready for readers to ponder, embrace, argue with, or reject as they choose.

Politics as Escapism

Friedman: You seem to be a proponent of filmmakers commenting on the political and social landscape (Mike Leigh being an example). Why do you think this is important? Why doesn't it take place more?

Carney: Hollywood separates personal and social issues because the producers are afraid of alienating anyone. They are salesmen, and every salesman knows better than to discuss religion or politics. You might lose a customer if you actually took a stand on anything that mattered. The reviewers go along with the whole thing because reviewing, at least here in America, is a form of advertising and advertisements never propose changing anything more radical than the brand of beer you drink for fear someone might disagree with them. If a reviewer actually took a stand on something, he or she would be accused of being biased. Remember Antonioni's description of Hollywood? "Being nowhere, saying nothing, about no one." Well, it's still true about both Hollywood and the review machine that supports and promotes it.

But don't get me wrong. Movies that puff themselves up with a lot of political and sociological heavy-breathing, like the ones Oliver Stone and Michael Moore make, are not necessarily any better than the Blonde Leading the Blonde ones. Politics can be a form of escapism too. Stone's and Moore's social critiques let us run away from our own lives. Their hell has other people in it. The problems they describe are always caused by someone else. Not by you and me. We know that can't be true since the world is made up of yous and mes. There's no one else. Our leaders may be shallow, but we elected them. Our culture may be organized around competition and greed, but we are the ones who buy all those SUVs and fight for that promotion at work. TV programs and Super Bowl ads may be stupid, but they wouldn't be on if we didn't watch them and buy the products they sell.

Great art doesn't point its finger at someone else. It asks people to examine their own lives, to look into their own hearts and minds. [Laughs and does a voice:] "Oh, I'm sorry, I don't have time for that. I don't want to miss an episode of *Desperate Housewives.*"

If you want an example of how a movie can be political without shifting the blame to someone else or treating its characters as victims of some impersonal "system," look at Todd Haynes's *Safe*. It never preaches or attitudinizes about social problems. But it reveals that the way the world is organized and understood affects the smallest individual acts. It makes us think deeply about the connections between culture and individuals—about how we structure our lives, about our desire for order and clarity, about our fear of what we can't control. It shows that the personal is political and the political is personal. That's what makes it one of the most subversive and radical American films of the past ten years. Robert Kramer and Godfrey Reggio and Jay Rosenblatt are other filmmakers who avoid the blame game.

Friedman: *Why do you think film critics don't usually put films within a political or social or economic context? Would it be helpful for them to do so?*

Carney: It's even weirder than that. If a film has the least bit of leftist political content, newspaper and magazine reviewers will jump up and down on it for being "biased" or "slanted." But when a mainstream Hollywood movie is practically a feature-length ad in praise of the NRA, foreign adventurism, or some other right-wing insanity, the reviewers don't notice that it has any politics at all. If Robert Kramer's *Milestones* or Barbara Trent's *Panama Deception* dares to suggest that there might be something wrong with America's foreign policy, Tony Scott [at *The New York Times*] will object that it is too "political." Meanwhile The Rock or Vin Diesel can use a bazooka to blow away every mustachioed man in the Middle East and Scott never raises an eyebrow.

Directors and films are only accused of being "political" if their politics differs from that of the Rotary Club. If their stupidity coincides with the idiocy of the White House, they are not considered biased. It's no different from the way Ralph Nader's political campaign is denied news coverage and Noam Chomsky is accused of being a conspiracy theorist while Charlie Rose, who functions as a publicity flack for every rich and powerful businessman in America, is treated as if he and his guests were distinguished intellectuals. The moral is obvious. If you want to get on *Charlie Rose* or be interviewed by *The New York Times*, don't question the corrupt, compromised, self-serving status quo. If you do, they'll call you "politically motivated." You don't get to be a movie reviewer at a place like *The Times* if you have a history of rocking the boat. Can you imagine them appointing someone as a lead reviewer who had a track record of having pointed out the reactionary nature of Spielberg's work?

The System Is Broken

Friedman: Why is rocking the boat bad?

Carney: Reviewers have internalized Hollywood's fantasy island view of expression. They don't want to grapple with movies that have anything to do with the world or viewers' real lives. They might upset you. You might not be able to sleep that night. You might have to do something in response. That would be to take movies entirely more seriously than these reviewers do. It wouldn't be "just a movie" anymore.

Am I being too harsh? I don't think so. Why do even so-called quality magazines and newspapers spend months covering the Academy Awards, which is nothing more than a big, self-congratulatory company picnic that screens a lot of bad film clips? When was the last time a real work of art even got nominated as Best Picture? Every week in my independent film course I show movies most people have never heard of that are better than any American movie that has ever won an Academy Award. If there is any press coverage criticizing the nominees, it's confined to stupidity like whether *A Beautiful Mind* played a little loose with the facts or Mel Gibson's *Passion* is historically accurate. Where are all the articles protesting that *Sink or Swim* didn't get nominated for Best Picture the year it was made? That *Koyaanisqatsi* didn't? That *Ice* didn't? That *Wanda* didn't? That *What Happened Was* didn't? That *Safe* didn't? That *Killer of Sheep* didn't? That *Girlfriends* didn't? That *Mikey and Nicky* didn't? That *Little Stiff* didn't? That *Human Remains* didn't?

The whole reviewing system is broken. Or hopelessly corrupt. Movie reviewers want you to think that they are functioning the same way as music or art critics, but they're actually just an extension of the Hollywood PR machine. Film reviewers, even at tony places like *The New York Times* and *Time* magazine, are publicity flacks for the studios and the DVD releasing companies. I heard a media critic bemoaning the fact that 80 percent of what appears in the daily newspaper is the product of government and corporate press releases. Well, I have news for him. When it comes to film coverage, forget about that twenty percent of original research. Film coverage in *The Times* or *Newsweek* or *Time* magazine is 100 percent the product of press releases!

The Culture of Unreality

Friedman: What's wrong with using press releases as the basis for a story?

Carney: Well you could say that it means that you can buy your way into the paper. The news becomes a form of advertising. The culture of salesmanship bleeds out of the ads and into the stories. The newspaper is no longer a chronicle of the most important events and opinions; it becomes a record of what money and power, the corporate publicists and press officers with the most cultural clout want you to know and believe.

But that's not really an adequate description of the scope of the problem. The situation we are in is actually much stranger and more disturbing. "Fact" and "fiction" are no longer separate realms. We live in a culture of unreality where the news—and much else—is part of some third realm of synthetic reality. Fiction has become fact.

It's why it's so comical when journalists beat their breasts over Jason Blair's fabrications or Dan Rather's reporting on Bush's National Guard service or Colin Powell's claims that Iraq had weapons of mass destruction—as if anything else in *The Times* or on *The Evening News* had a different epistemological status.

It seems a bit late in the day for reporters to be wringing their hands over there being no there there, particularly since they helped create the situation they are bemoaning. For more than five decades the news has consisted almost entirely of simulated facts, imitation events, pseudo-drama—from the juvenile delinquency crisis and the Red menace of the 1950s, to the missile gap and the Chinese threat in the 1960s, to the Moral Majority, the Reagan revolution, Newt Gingrich's contract with America, the Whitewater scandal, the Segway personal transportation breakthrough, O.J.'s guilt, the war on terrorism, Janet Jackson's breast, and the liberation of Iraq. Every item in this list of so-called events, crises, and confrontations—and a thousand others that get onto the pages of our newspapers every day—is equally a fiction, part of the history of style, something that belongs on the fashion pages. There's no difference between Terry Schiavo's smile and the smile of the winner of *American Idol*. We've woken up in Nabokov's dream. Our "reality" has quotation marks around it.

You know the postmodern transformation is a *fait accompli* when the physicists have become part of it—fighting to get tenure with versions of string theory—rival sets of equations whose only verifiable result is their ability to get coverage on the front page of *The Times*.

Hollywood loves this confusion of realms, this funhouse-mirror mix-up of events and unrealities, of course. It's a publicist's meat and potatoes. It does their work for them. They spend a lot of money trying to blur the distinction between facts and fictions for reporters, readers, and viewers, so that the reverence and importance that attaches to the Holocaust or D-Day or Christianity will be attached to the fictional depictions in movies like *Schindler's List, Saving Private Ryan,* and *The Passion of the Christ.*

Friedman: What can be done?

Carney: I don't know. Maybe nothing. It has been going on for so long that it may be too late to change it. America has sung and danced its way pretty far down the yellow brick road to Oz by now. It just might come apart at the seams in another decade or two. That might actually be a good thing. For the rest of the world, I mean.

If you want to see films that deal with this confusion of facts and fictions— and the fabricated nature even of our emotional realities—look at Mark Rappaport's movies. Maybe that's why *The Times* doesn't do feature pieces on him. [Laughs] It would blow their cover. Though more likely he's shut out because he can't afford to hire a publicist to issue press releases that masquerade as news, or hold press conferences to redefine his fictions as historical events, the way Spielberg does.

Printing the Press Release

Someone who opens *The Times* film section thinks they are reading news— factually correct, objective, unbiased news stories—or, in the case of an opinion piece, a frank, uncoerced, candid personal viewpoint, when they are actually reading advertising. The only reason we don't detect how weird this is because so many of our values are already skewed in the same way television and the newspapers are. Since that de-realized Rappaportian third realm is where most of our lives are already lived, we don't really notice it when we encounter it in the media. Money, power, celebrity, and gossip define so much of our culture that we can't see how crazy it is to let them define the news as well.

You want an example? Although I gave up reading *The Times* movie coverage on a regular basis years ago, because of my interest in John Cassavetes, a friend sent me a piece published about him in September 2004. It was written by Manohla Dargis, one of the paper's lead film reporters. It was a retrospective appreciation of Cassavetes' work. Now, anyone reading the article would assume two things: first, that it was motivated sheerly out of respect for Cassavetes' films and a desire to pay homage to them; and, second, that it represented a more or less objective, noncommercial treatment of the subject.

Well, since I happen to know this particular subject inside-out, I can tell you categorically that neither thing was true. First, Dargis's article wasn't a disinterested homage. It was part of the publicity campaign for a Cassavetes DVD box set being issued that same month. It was prompted by and based on a press release issued by the company promoting the set. Second, the article was full of distortions and errors, of both omission and commission, which systematically suppressed a series of embarrassing facts connected with the decision-making process behind the set and what it included. I happen to know that part of the story since I was personally involved in it as the set's scholarly advisor. It's told on my Cassavetes.com website. There's not a whisper of any of that in what Dargis wrote. The controversy about the set's content and creation was totally suppressed.

Now if that's an example of the work of the person who holds the most prestigious film reviewing job in America, whose copy is overseen by the most highly-respected editors in all of journalism, and is published in "the newspaper of record"—that the story she filed was part of a PR campaign for a DVD release and that it was tailored to promote the product by saying only favorable things about it and avoiding raising embarrassing issues.... well, I'll leave it to your imagination what goes on at places like *Premiere* and *Entertainment Tonight*.

The film reviewers might as well be working for the studios and DVD releasers. In fact many of them are. Roger Ebert often reviews and promotes DVD disks which he has been involved with the production of.

But the problem is larger than that one tiny piece of the pie. Virtually everybody in the reviewing game is in bed with everybody on the promotional side of things. The publicists invent phony behind-the-scenes drama, feed the reviewers fictional celebrity gossip, and fly them out to LA on all-expense-paid junkets to interview the stars—and a week or two later the reviewers dutifully report the fictions in the forms of articles, interviews, and reviews. PR becomes news. When the White House tries to manipulate reporters this way, the Washington press corps at least puts up a token struggle. But when the studios do this to the reviewers, the only complaints they ever get are that the hotel rooms are not fancy enough or that the plane tickets are not first class. No one writing about film for a major publication dares to say how corrupt the whole system is for fear that they will be expelled from the club and be denied the next big interview or photo op with the next big nobody.

I heard Stanley Tucci talk about this a while ago. He was on a panel discussing the problems that confront filmmakers who attempt to do artistic work. Everyone else was blaming the studios, the budgets, the cost of special effects, the distributors, the movie theaters. He said wait a minute, the main reason our movies are so stupid is because our reviewers are. He talked about how bad reviewing in America is, how it panders to mass entertainment notions, how it sucks up to movie stars, how every reviewer in America reviews the same five Hollywood releases every week, how none of them supports art. I almost fell off my chair. It was the first time I ever heard anyone ever publicly cite reviewers as the problem. Most actors and directors will say it in private, but they are afraid to say it in public for fear of having Anthony Lane or David Denby retaliate in a review. Tucci's point was that we're not going to have audiences for good films until we have reviewers who write about good films. If you're an indie, you can get all the distribution you want, but if reviewers don't review your work and encourage people to see it, only you and your friends will be in the theaters watching it.

But, if we're playing Pin the Tail on the Donkey, we need to take a good hard look at ourselves too. Just as is the case with political leaders and hit television shows, we ultimately get the reviewers and films we deserve. If people really cared about seeing great films, they'd boo bad movies or storm out of them and ask for their money back or stop mobbing celebrity events with Renee Zellweger and Ben Stiller. As long as we keep shelling out money to see junk, junk is what we're going to get. That's how capitalism and democracy work. Or don't work. Look at who's in the White House. Democracy is in even worse shape than film reviewing! [Laughs] I guess I shouldn't be laughing. It's not funny. Our culture is very sick. In very serious trouble.

Distortions of Democratic Values

Friedman: Why do you think reviewers are not more supportive of artistic work?

Carney: The basic problem is our culture's love affair with money and power and publicity. The celebrity suck-up factor is the most blatant manifestation of it, since celebrities represent all three realms. They are rich; they are powerful; and they are famous. Actors and directors are the American royalty. Everyone wants to interview them or write about them and is afraid to say anything negative for fear of alienating them. When was the last time Terry Gross or Barbara Walters or Charlie Rose laid into Tom Hanks or Steven Spielberg for the meretriciousness of their work? Of course, the real problem is that Gross and Walters and Rose don't even see that their work is stupid, because they are so awed that they are interviewing celebrities.

The flip side is that if you make a work of art that doesn't have a movie star in it and doesn't have a PR office promoting it—in other words, if it isn't wildly popular or on the way to being wildly popular, as works of art generally are not—it won't be valued by the culture. Blame it on democracy. We're so deep into a view of life as being measured in terms of success and popularity that we've forgotten that art can't be evaluated this way.

We have to remember how weird it is to do this. It's really crazy. Spiritual and moral values that mattered for thousands of years have been replaced by commercial evaluations. Instead of writing articles and having discussions about a work's truth, its morality, its ability to inspire us or make us think, reviewers and commentators focus on the size of its budget, its box office revenues, its demographic. Questions about what is right or wrong, good or bad have been replaced by discussions of what's "hot," what had the biggest opening weekend, what is generating the biggest "buzz." It's a PR view of life.

The emphasis on race, class, gender, and ideology in the classroom is an expression of the same way of viewing experience as if it were measurable and quantifiable. Moral questions about the degree of love and nobility in a work give way to political calculations about whether it is "representative," "inclusive," "ideologically correct," or—God help us—"offensive," "objectionable," or "insulting." Sociology replaces philosophy.

This force field distorts every area of film appreciation and study: the books that get published, the articles that get written, what is taught in our universities, what is screened at events.

Friedman: Can you say more about that?

Carney: There's too much to say! [Laughing] Neither of us will live long enough. Let me start with film festivals. The very reason they exist supposedly is to celebrate the art of film—in other words to offer an alternative to the culture of popularity, PR, and hype; but instead they attempt to play the same game as the rest of the culture, programming their event schedules and ceremonies around celebrity appearances, movie star awards, saturation press coverage, and big ticket sales—which means that if a film doesn't have a name director or actor attached to it, it gets relegated to a Tuesday morning screening. What's the reason for a film festival to exist if it's going to organize its opening and closing night events around Academy Awards values and celebrity appearances by Julia Roberts and George Clooney?

Even the so-called indie festivals are corrupted by the same PR understanding of life. I was reminded of this not too long ago. I got a note from a programmer who said he was thinking about inviting Rob Nilsson as a guest of honor. Present a retrospective of his work and give him some kind of award. But the programmer wanted to check with me whether I thought Nilsson's films would be a hit with the audience. If they weren't, he said he didn't want to go through with the invitation. I guess you could say I lost my cool. I told him that Nilsson had been busting his chops on the fringes for something like thirty years, bucking the system, financing films out of his own pocket, losing money, risking everything, and it was insulting and irrelevant to be grading him on whether or not his name or work would draw big audiences. I told the programmer he should become a Hollywood producer since he had mastered the Hollywood way of thinking. He replied—and I'm sure he thought he was being extremely reasonable and that I was the nut case— that he couldn't possibly invite someone if his work wouldn't get favorable reviews from local reviewers and draw decent-sized audiences. So that's what it comes down to, even at a small, prestigious festival nominally committed to indie film. The programmers make the same commercial calculations as your local metroplex. If the know-nothing reviewer for the local paper doesn't like Rob Nilsson's work, or hasn't heard of him, you don't invite Rob Nilsson.

I saw the same thing happen when I was on the advisory board of the Boston Film Festival. I quit in disgust after about ten years of it. The most important reviewer in the city at that point was... Jay Carr. At that time he was the lead reviewer for the *Boston Globe*, but he has since moved on to being a television film reviewer... Well, year after year, we would sit around a table at meetings debating whether we should invite so-and-so or program such-and-such based on our guesses about "whether Jay would cover the event" or "what kind of review Jay would give it." His opinion affected every decision.

The second worst Boston film critic at the time was a guy named David Brudnoy. He... did less damage because he wrote for a less important paper, something called *The Tab*. The festival took a different tack with him. They appointed him to the advisory board and let him have input into the decision-making process! [Laughs] Isn't that clever? Isn't that sicko? Do I have to point the moral and adorn the tale by telling you that, as it sailed between the critical Scylla of Carr and the Charybdis of Brudnoy, the festival ended up giving an award to a bimbo movie star year after year? Surprise, surprise. Capitalism triumphs again.

Celebrity Worship

Friedman: But festivals do have to support themselves through ticket sales.

Carney: Yes, but economics are not what is driving these decisions. I am talking about values and the effects of values are subtler and more insidious. The world we have inside us is our real undoing. It's much a more powerful determiner of actions than the world outside. Economics may be the reason these programmers give for their decisions, but they are not really forced to do what they do by economic pressures. The worship of fame and celebrity and money, the measurement of things in terms of buzz and ticket sales and press coverage and favorable reviews is inside us—even if we don't realize it. That internal slavery is our undoing.

Think about public institutions like libraries and museums. They don't have to support their operations through box office receipts, but they are no different. They host the same movie-star awards ceremonies, the same opening night galas, the same name directors and films as commercial film festivals do. The awe of celebrities, the desire to please them and get favorable write-ups in the newspaper goes so deep in our culture and is so much part of the internal values of a programmer or curator, that there is no difference if the organization is a commercial one or a non-profit.

It's not economics, it's values. I had first-hand experience of that a few years ago. I discovered a new version of one of John Cassavetes' films in the Library of Congress. It was a major find. The Motion Picture Division archivists were excited. I made plans with them to issue an announcement, hold a press conference, and conduct a screening. So far so good. Then Cassavetes' widow, Gena Rowlands, told the staff she was opposed to it. As far as I can determine, it appears that she was afraid that if the new version became known it would cut into rentals of the old version.
Well, if I was under any illusion that the Library of Congress served the interest of the public, and was above being manipulated by a celebrity, it ended that day. Rowlands had no legal or moral control over what the Library did with the print, but the Library of Congress curator instantly agreed to her request that the discovery be suppressed. At the same time, probably at her request, he refused to tell me what was going on. I kept waiting for the announcement and screening we had planned. When I called or wrote to ask why it wasn't being scheduled, he wouldn't reply.

When I later learned what had taken place, at first I couldn't believe it. I thought it must have all been a miscommunication. I had thought the Library of Congress existed strictly to further the scholarship and appreciation of its collection. I had thought my tax dollars went to supporting an institution devoted to making available the greatest and best works of the past.

Now I realize how naïve I was. Gena Rowlands told them to jump through her hoops, and the only question they asked was how high. [Does a voice:] "She's a famous movie star, for gosh sake! What part of 'yes, ma'am' don't you understand?" Wealth, power, and celebrity set the agenda in those hallowed halls just as much as they do everywhere else in American culture. It has nothing to do with economics or money. In fact, in this particular case, the Library of Congress forfeited the potential box office receipts from the screening of the new film to keep a movie star happy. The administrators at the Library of Congress are as in awe of celebrity as some small-town jour-nalist. For the record, I made that discovery three years ago. To this day, no announcement has been issued and no screenings have been held.

When I started out, I used to imagine that scholarly publishing operated outside the system of fad and hype. Well, that may be true in terms of phi-losophy and mathematics and physics, but it's sure not the case with film books. What gets published by scholarly presses is dictated by the same forces as what is promoted in the culture. If something is popular, if some-thing is newsworthy, if it appeals to a particular demographic—gays, African Americans, World War II veterans, holocaust survivors, or whatever—that's what gets published.

I learned that early on when I sent out the manuscript of my first book. It was about Cassavetes and was turned down everywhere, even though each editor said the writing was fine. Each one told me the problem was that Cassavetes didn't have a following. I remember the exact words of one of them: "If it were Woody Allen, it would be different. But it's Cassavetes. He's just not a household name." Can you imagine refusing to consider a manuscript about Heidegger or Riemann or Planck because they are not Woody Allen; because they are not household names?

Well, it's now twenty years later, and Cassavetes has become fashionable. So now it's easy to get something published about him. But why should pop-ularity matter—either way—then or now? And what about a current Cassavetes who is not a household name?

The non-academic film book situation is even worse. Publishers are almost exclusively committed to publishing books that tie-in with PR events: a new DVD box set, the re-release of a film, the twenty-fifth anniversary of some-thing or other. It's the film book as product tie-in. [Laughs] Move over McDonalds and Burger King.

One of the dirty secrets of film book publishing is that a good fraction of it is subsidized by big name directors and stars, who commission books about their own work, paying authors to publish favorable critical studies. You heard it here first. I'm not sure the publishers realize what is going on. The only reason I know this happens is that I have friends who have written such books. It goes a long way toward explaining why there are so many books on some of these actors and directors. From the filmmaker's or movie star's perspective, it makes financial sense. Getting a book published about your work is an excellent investment—given the size of a movie budget, an extremely cheap one—with a potentially enormous payback. For less than $50,000 you can get a book written and published about you that can increase the box office value of your work by tens of millions.

It works the other way too. Things are taken out of books if they might offend a movie star. You can't really say negative things about Martin Scorsese, Peter Bogdanovich, Sundance, or the AFI [American Film Institute] without facing repercussions. I've had passages in my writing removed by editors afraid of alienating a powerful director or star "who has helped us in the past and who we are counting on for a jacket blurb." Of course I squawk, but the editor usually prevails. If I really dig in my heels, they can always play their trump card and tell you the lawyers won't allow it because of a potential lawsuit. But no matter what you call it, it's still censorship.

Truth and Consequences

Friedman: I'm glad you fight it.

Carney: Look, I have it pretty easy. I'm a teacher. I have a job that pays me a salary. I don't depend on currying favor with movie stars to make my living. I can take the consequences.

Friedman: What do you mean by consequences?

Carney: It's not nursery school. The system retaliates. Studios, publicists, movie stars, and magazines don't take criticism lying down. If a television or magazine reviewer bashes Vin Diesel or Tom Hanks, she won't be allowed an interview with him on the next publicity junket, and will get in trouble with her editor or producer and ultimately be out of a job. That's the way the system works. If Charlie Rose started asking hard questions, if he were less sycophantic, a lot of big name guests wouldn't agree to appear on his show.

I remember an editor warning me about how things worked back at the beginning of my career. Leon Wieseltier at *The New Republic* asked me if I'd be willing to write a piece about the awfulness of film reviewing in *The New York Times*. I said I'd love to do it. Since I was just out of grad school, young and dumb, he must have felt sorry for me, so he warned me about the consequences. He said the only reason he was asking me was that he had approached a string of established writers and all of them had turned him down because they didn't want the *Times* to blackball their next book. To give it a bad review or—what's worse, no review. They couldn't afford the repercussions.

It's not just the *Times* of course. After I wrote something about the shallowness of *Film Comment*, which I had written for prior to that, the editor wrote me and told me he would make sure I never got anything printed in the magazine again. That was ten or fifteen years ago, and guess what? I haven't.

There are a number of reviewers who gun for me and bash my work because of things that I have said about them. And both Pauline Kael and Gena Rowlands have threatened to sue me because they didn't like things that I have written or posted on my web site. And Rowlands also got me fired from a job.

Friedman: I know the Rowlands story since it's on your Cassavetes.com web site, but what happened with Kael?

Carney: I wrote an essay criticizing her writing, so she had her lawyer call me up and "talk to me." It was a scene out of *The Godfather.* [Laughs] As with any threat of legal action, you don't actually need to take the person to court to have an effect. The threat itself is enough to scare the daylights out of someone in my income bracket. Kael and Rowlands in effect put me on notice that it would cost me a thousand dollars an hour for every hour after that that they chose to make my life miserable. That's what high-powered lawyers charge. If that isn't enough to get you to pull your article or make the changes someone is demanding, it sure makes you think twice before you say or write anything negative again.

Friedman: What did you say was wrong with Kael's writing?

Carney: I basically said it was stupid. I said her reviews were a series of dictional and metaphorical stunts. A lot of flashy metaphors, name-dropping allusions, kicky, campy, odd-ball diction. Glitz and glitter. Snap, crackle, and pop. In-jokes and tippy-toe verbal pirouettes. Entertaining but empty. And, most importantly, simply wrong, wrong, wrong about virtually every film she ever reviewed. Does anyone still think that *The Godfather and Dressed to Kill* and *Blue Velvet* and *Bonnie and Clyde* are the life-changing experiences she said they were? The greatest expressions of which the human spirit is capable?

But, boy, was she influential. She died a few years ago but she's still very much with us. Verbally I mean. I could rattle off the names of twenty major reviewers who have cloned her style. Paulettes, a friend of mine calls them. Many of them were actual acolytes. They came to her apartment, sat at her feet and worshipped her, and she got them their jobs. They keep the votive candles burning brightly. You should have heard them waxing poetic about her genius on film festival panels the year after she died. *The New Yorker*'s David Denby is probably the best known of the bunch. For four or five years at the *Times* Elvis Mitchell did a pretty good imitation of her style—her verbal pyrotechnics, slumming low-brow references, and devotion to Hollywood values. He actually used to cite her as the inspiration for a lot of his work. Anthony Lane at the *New Yorker* is another younger-generation acolyte. There is always a market for bad writing, lack of discernment, and show-boating, and there are always readers ready to be taken in by it. In the culture that brings you the Super Bowl halftime show and the Academy Awards, flash passes for importance. Stylishness masquerades as substance. We've forgotten how to tell the difference. The writing of Lane and Mitchell is much admired.

Corporate Consumer Culture

Friedman: What is your biggest gripe with most film criticism today?

Carney: As my secretary says, "Don't get me started!" Since we haven't got a week, I'll have to give you a short list of some of the most obvious lunacy:

Let's begin with the fact that Hollywood movies get reviewed in the first place. You know, only about one book out of a hundred ever gets even a single-sentence mention in the *Times*, but every Hollywood movie is guaranteed a review—and often more than that: a review, a feature piece, an interview with the star, and then another interview with the director. What does that tell you about the power of the advertising tail to wag the editorial dog?

On the other hand, if film reviewers are going to let the advertisers dictate what they write about, why not at least call a spade a spade? Why don't

they tell the truth? Why don't they say: "This movie was planned and produced to cash in on a trendy social issue to generate publicity; it features a
big name star to suck in viewers and generate media interviews; and it
pushes a few non-threatening emotional buttons but leaves everything
unchanged in the end in order to give people a feel-good experience that
will encourage people to recommend it to their friends." Why not call the
garbage garbage? When was the last time a movie reviewer wrote what is
obvious about ninety-nine out of a hundred movies? That they were made
for morons. That they pander to our basest desires. That they are machines
for flattery?

I've already talked about the shameless celebrity worship in the media. Are
we all still star-struck teenagers? Isn't it time for an adult reality-check?
Why interview Ron Howard and Steven Spielberg about the art of film, as if
they were thinkers, and knew anything worth imparting? Why do Charlie
Rose and James Lipton fawn on Harrison Ford and Julia Roberts, treating
them as if they were actors? Why are movie stars never asked a single hard
question by an interviewer—like why they are wasting their lives making
junky movies? No, why spoil the party? It's more fun to sit around and yuk it
up about how great it was to make *Ocean's Eleven*. But enough about journalists! Since I'm a professor, I'll give you two academic pet peeves:

First, I'm fed up with writers in the *New York Review of Books* who try to
redeem crummy movies by finding grandiose metaphors and themes in them
or intricate re-workings of genre conventions. You know, the ones that
argue that *Showgirls* is profound because it depicts the commodification of
American life, or that no matter how trite and formulaic *Artificial
Intelligence* is, we have to take it seriously since it is freighted with
metaphoric significance. Give me a break. The movie becomes a jungle gym
for the critic to do his intellectual gymnastic spins and twirls on. Not one
viewer in a thousand gets these sorts of meanings from these movies, and,
if you catch them in private, the filmmakers themselves will tell you that
they don't understand a word the critic wrote.

Even if this were what viewers were getting from these works, there is
something wrong with such a high degree of abstraction. These critics pitch
their tents in some Joseph Campbell heaven of symbolic references, thirty
thousand feet above the actual experience of life. There is something
screwed up about a critic who cares more about archetypal themes than
individual feelings and experiences, just as there was something fundamentally wrong with Joseph Campbell's understanding of life. As Orwell put it,

there are some ideas so stupid only a professor could believe them.

Second, I'm exasperated with professors who attempt to justify their interest in junky TV shows and movies with theories about how they matter because so many people go to them and so much money is spent on them. If they're going to pursue that line of reasoning with any consistency, they should stop discussing films and start analyzing video games in their classes. There's much more money spent on them in any given year than on movies. The music department should stop listening to Bach and Mozart and start playing music by Brittany and J. Lo. The drama department should stop *reading Chekhov and Tennessee Williams and start doing scenes from Chorus Line* and *Phantom of the Opera.* The English department should bump Chaucer and Milton and start having students write papers on Tom Clancy and Steven King.

Professors will tell you that movie culture is to the twentieth- and twenty-first century what folk culture was for preceding centuries. Two hundred years ago people had quilting bees, whaling voyage scrimshaw, and county fairs; we have Steven Spielberg, *The Matrix, Austin Powers*, and Sponge Bob. What's the difference? But the equivalence of the two realms is founded on a conceptual fallacy. It ignores the fundamental differences between folk art and the creations of the corporate mass media.

Folk art is the expression of the daily lives of ordinary people. It encodes deep, enduring social, historical, and spiritual values. The creations of folk traditions are not mass-produced and generic, but hand-made, hand-crafted, individual, unique objects and activities created for particular uses and occasions. Their aesthetic is conservative. It doesn't change every month or year. Folk art represents an alternative to commercial systems of understanding and measurement. Its value is measured not in terms of popularity and profitability, but in terms of functionality, meaning, and attractiveness.

Contemporary American popular art—including Hollywood film—is the opposite. It is not a deep cultural expression of spiritual values. The creations of media corporations—from movies to TV shows and commercials to product tie-ins—are expressions of business values. They are mass-produced industrial products, designed to be hawked on every corner, grab as much momentary attention as possible, and make as much money as they can before the next big thing comes along. They don't encapsulate deep cultural feelings and attitudes. They are not anchored in peoples' unique experiences and histories. They do not express spiritual values. These creations rely on flash, glitz, and glitter. They are part of the worship of newness. They deny the past in the interest of celebrating an ever-changing present. They are designed and marketed within the advertising system to be replaced by the next item in an infinite cycle of planned obsolescence and disposability.

The professors couldn't be more wrong. The two kinds of culture are not equivalent. Corporate consumer culture is a betrayal of everything folk culture represents.

Youth Culture and Mature Culture

Friedman: But Hollywood film is an important cultural phenomenon, particularly for young people. They attend movies in large numbers and think of their lives in terms of them.

Carney: Even kids don't take most movies that seriously. A lot of their attendance has nothing to do with the movie itself. When they're standing in line to see *Austin Powers*, they're there less for the movie than the event. It's about dressing up, getting out of the house, and having the experience of hanging out with your friends. It's not that different from why some adults go to Broadway plays. It's not really about the work. It's about having a social experience you can feel part of and talk with your friends about the next day.

But I'll admit that there are a few movies every year—*The Royal Tennenbaums*, *The Matrix* and *Titanic* are examples—that do matter intensely to young people. It's an adolescent experimentation and identification thing. The films that young people go to are always about young people's lives, and young people go to them to see themselves in them, to compare their lives with those of the characters, to have experiences they can't have in their real lives. But, in either instance, my point is that the film experience is an expression of youth culture—not mature culture. When we talk about the mystique and popularity of film, we have to remember that we're talking about its appeal to young people almost exclusively. When these same people graduate, get a full-time job, or start raising a family, they stop going to these sorts of movies and often stop going to movies altogether. That doesn't happen with real art. You don't stop caring about it when you turn thirty.

Friedman: Why is that?

Carney: The shallowness of the experiences these movies offer almost guarantees that they will seem silly to an adult. They are children's movies. Like children's books, they can't sustain adult interests. They are not made for adults, but for teenagers and others in various states of arrested development—like film reviewers.

It's telling that most Americans over the age of 40 don't go to the movies, and the ones that do don't take them as serious expressions of anything! It's easy for reviewers and film professors to forget this. Even I forget it sometimes. But you get a reminder at Thanksgiving or Christmas when you discover that your aunts and uncles and cousins have never even heard of *American Beauty* or *Magnolia* or *Mulholland Drive* or the Coen brothers or Harmony Korine or Robert Bresson and have absolutely no interest in finding out who or what they are. If you put one of these videos in the VCR, they leave the room.

That's why the parents of most of my students think they are wasting their time majoring in film. As far as they are concerned, it's a phase their kids are going through. In their view, movies are escapist trash. No one in their right mind would take them seriously. I try to keep that in mind when I'm teaching film. It's a good corrective to prevent me from waxing poetic about cinema as the twentieth- or twenty-first-century art form. Not to these realtor mothers and businessman fathers! [Laughs]

Now I don't agree with those parents about most other things, but you know, even from where I sit, it's clear that movies are not the great contemporary art form, and anyone who says they are is only showing his ignorance of other art. If you want to talk about enduring artistic value in terms of English-language work, the short stories of the past century are a thousand times deeper and artistically more important than the films. D.H. Lawrence and Eudora Welty and Alice Munro and Joyce Carol Oates have done more in a single book of stories than David Cronenberg and Steven Spielberg have done in their entire careers. Heck, I'll go further. Any one of their short stories is more complex than any feature film that has ever won the Best Picture Award. Tell that to Charlie Rose.

Friedman: Do you see any indications of an alternative critical community evolving to counter what you see in the mainstream press?

Carney: I just don't know. The artists are the only critics I really trust. If Caveh Zahedi or Tom Noonan or Jay Rosenblatt tells me something is worth seeing, I'll walk barefoot over broken glass to get to it. I guess my hope is that some of my own students will change the history of film criticism in the next fifteen years. But I'll have to wait and see if that happens. It doesn't seem very likely. All the odds are stacked against it.

What is Art?

Friedman: What qualities must a filmmaker embody to be an artist?

Carney: All that matters is that you tell your own personal truth. That you present some aspect of experience the way you see and feel it. Not the way anyone else does. Not the way any other movie has ever shown it. There is no right or wrong way to do it. Your movie can take a trillion unknown, undiscovered forms. It can be about anything. Showing us how strange and miraculous our lives are. How weird society is. How extraordinary ordinary people are. How revelatory everyday life can be. It can depict the love and kindness that never make the news. Or the mystery of what we are. The important thing is to copy no one. Forget every film you've ever seen, everything you've been taught in film school. That's why film school is a curse. It teaches you to become an imitator, but the one thing we know for sure is that the next great work of art won't look at all like the last one. I don't want to see another *Citizen Kane*. I saw that movie already. My students are always recommending something they think I'll admire because it's "like Tarkovsky" or some other filmmaker whose work I show in class. But I don't want a filmmaker who makes Cassavetes or Leigh or Ozu or Tarkovsky movies. Those filmmakers didn't become who they were by imitating someone else, but by throwing their feelings and insights up on screen in their own unique ways.

Friedman: What directors in Hollywood are making films that transcend the studio mindset?

Carney: I would be the last to know. Or care. It's like asking who worked for Enron but transcended the corporate mindset? There might have been someone, but the question then would be why he worked for Enron. Why not ask what non-Hollywood directors transcend the studio mindset? There are amazing artists out there, but you aren't going to see their faces on the cover of the next issue of Premiere. Every week I get videos in the mail from filmmakers I've never heard of whose work is better than what is playing in the mall. Let me give you some names of the great contemporary

American filmmakers: Fran Rizzo, Andrew Bujalski, Jay Rosenblatt, Sam Seder, Su Friedrich, Charles Burnett, Mark Rappaport, Vince Gallo, Tom Noonan, John O'Brien, Chris Brown, Jim McKay, Rob Nilsson, Harmony Korine, Larry Holden, Chris Smith, Gordon Erikson, Paul Harrill, Josh Apter, David Ball, Terry Zwigoff, Joe Berlinger, Bruce Sinofsky, Caveh Zahedi, Rick Schmidt, Jim Jarmusch, Eric Mendelsohn, David Barker. I'm sure there are dozens of others I'm forgetting to mention or don't know about. Never heard of most of them? That just proves my point. It's the hacks whose names are on every tongue, whose faces are everywhere, who are profiled in the *Times*. Here's a rule of thumb: if someone is on *Charlie Rose,* you can be absolutely, positively sure they don't really matter.

Darkness Visible

Friedman: Why do you think there has been a trend of anti-sentimental films in recent years?

Carney: The epilogue to my Leigh book talks about this. It's a way of bursting the bubble, of revealing that the empress is wearing a pushup bra. Black comedy surfaces when options for truth-telling are blocked or frustrated. Society always tries to paper over its imaginative San Andreas faults. One of the jobs of an artist is to reveal the gaps and inconsistencies in the cultural cover story. Artists have been doing this for centuries. In the expansionist, optimistic, go-go Elizabethan period—so much like our own Wall Street greed-crazed Reagan-Bush years—Kyd and Marlowe wrote these brilliant, dark, sardonic comedies—*Tamburlaine, The Jew of Malta, The Spanish Tragedy*. That was in 1590. At the height of the Eisenhower snooze-fest and the Kennedy-Camelot-preppie touch football game, Kubrick made *Paths of Glory* and *Dr. Strangelove*. In the peace-love-Woodstock era, Altman and Penn unleashed *Mash* and *Bonnie and Clyde*. Altman has been turning over Betsy Ross's stitching and forcing us to look at the bad side for more than thirty years. Someone has to do that from time to time.

Todd Solondz, Paul Thomas Anderson, Sam Mendez, and Neil LaBute flourish because they tell us something we need to hear. America is a relentlessly upbeat, optimistic culture. A sentimental culture with an immature view of life. Look at how 9/11 affected us. That's a sign of our immaturity. We see things in terms of black and white, good and evil, us versus them. These filmmakers correct our vision. They make the darkness visible.

They tell us that the dominant culture is screening out reality. They tell us that its mass-produced feel-good emotional costume jewelry is junk. That Hollywood is devoted to systematic, life-denying acts of repression. *Magnolia, American Beauty, Your Friends and Neighbors,* and *Happiness* are purgatives. Enemas to flush out the sentimental crap. Their causticness, irony, and satire are positive in this respect. They are the last refuge of the truth-telling, caring heart in hiding—forced underground by the happy-face fakery of American culture in the pre-9/11 decade.

But that doesn't mean these films are great works of art. I wouldn't say that of Marlowe's or Kyd's plays either. Shakespeare was the great artist of their era—because his art, like all great art, came out of love, trust, and sympathy, not sarcasm, illusion-shattering, and cynicism. The work of Altman, LaBute, Solondz, and the others is too purely negative. It isn't enough to show what is wrong. You have to find a way to affirm what is right, without denying what is. A lot of their work is mean-spirited, ungenerous, spiritually stingy, and emotionally closed. They take cheap shots. In other words, they are afraid. Before they can be real artists they have to risk more by loving more, or daring to show us what they love. That's dangerous for an artist. It's always easier to mock and sneer, particularly if your audience is people in their late teens and early twenties because satire is what they are most comfortable with at that age.

Punch Drunk Love is the one exception to what I am saying. It's Anderson's attempt to do what I'm asking for; but he can't pull it off. It's revealing that his attempt at a positive vision can only be done as a fairy tale.

It may sound paradoxical, but the anti-Hollywood perspective of these directors is actually evidence of their still being trapped in the Hollywood view of life. The anti-romanticism, the anti-sentimentality of *Magnolia, American Beauty,* and *Happiness* actually represents a nostalgia for old-fashioned romanticism and sentimentality. These anti-sentimental movies are actually sentimental at heart.

Friedman: *I don't see that. Can you explain what you mean?*

Carney: The anti-sentimental filmmakers look at movies like *Titanic* and *The Matrix* and note that the romantic idealism of their characters and the melodramatic intensifications of their events are false to what life really is. In reaction, they focus on the absence of romance in their characters' lives, the falsity of their idealistic understandings, and the fraudulence of their apparent virtue. Idealistic characters are shown to be deluded or revealed to be imposters. But to invert these values is really just to play the same game Hollywood plays, only upside down, inside out. Hollywood movies flatter us by telling us that we are visionary heroes; Solondz and LaBute and Paul Thomas Anderson reveal that we are frauds. Hollywood tells us we are angels; they tell us we are devils, cheats, scoundrels, or fools. But do you see what is going on? The anti-heroic stance of *Boogie Nights* and *Magnolia* and *Happiness* represents a perspective from within the heroic understanding of life. You haven't left the heroic paradigm behind; you are still inside it.

I'm not just playing games with terminology. *Magnolia* is as cloyingly, syrupily sentimental as *Titanic*. The narrative strategy of the film is to present larger-than-life images and then cut them down to size. A viewer is supposed to be moved by the difference between the grandiose, poised, or confident public image the character projects and his or her actual state of loneliness, emptiness, despair, or deceit. Narratively it's all a set-up. First you evoke the ideal and then you undermine it. The result is that you create this vague longing and nostalgia for the states of heroism and romantic connectedness even as you get credit for acknowledging their absence. But the romantic values you are undermining come from sentimental movies. They don't exist in life.

Sentimentality is any time you ask the viewer to feel something without forcing him to learn something. It's emotion without knowledge. Feeling without thinking. These movies are not about giving us new and complex understandings of their characters, but about making us feel sorry for them or, in a few cases, dislike them. That's too easy. It just substitutes one emotional cliché for another. Another reason to call them sentimental is that, just like Hollywood, they flatter the viewer.

Self–Pity

Friedman: How do these films flatter the viewer?

Carney: Films like *American Beauty, Magnolia, Boogie Nights, Happiness,* and *Welcome to the Dollhouse* plug into one of the main cultural archetypes of the MTV generation: a vision of young people as a group of walking-wounded betrayed by their parents, let down by their leaders, and damaged or broken by society, who either mope around feeling rejected, unwanted, lonely, and neglected—that's Paul Thomas Anderson's territory—or turn themselves into goof-ball nostalgics devoted to hanging-out together and recapturing the days of their youth in some kind of nonsexual family—that's Wes Anderson's.

This understanding of life is one of the recurring romantic myths—read early Byron, Eliot, or Truman Capote and you'll find it there—and it continues to snake its mournful, elegiac, nostalgic path through the pop-culture, twenty-something world of today. It's everywhere—in the music of Morrissey and Avril Lavigne, in the writing of Douglas Coupland, Nick Hornby, and Dave Eggers, and in these movies.

It's comforting because it lets the younger generation off the hook. Collapsing into an adolescent wail of despair or trying to recapture a golden age of childhood that never existed in the first place is just another form of escapism, another way of avoiding and denying the claims and complexities of adult life, another way of refusing to grow up. The young people in these films and the young people watching them wash their hands of the problems of adult society and console themselves that they are the hapless victims of even more screwed-up parents. They can blame their father, mother, or other authority figure for their problems. It's flattering because it allows young viewers or listeners to cast themselves as and to identify with all of the other damaged, weak, heartbroken misfits. In a word, it allows the viewer, listener, or reader to feel sorry for himself: "Oh, it's so hard to be born into a world where there are no more heroes, where everyone is flawed, where eternal love is no longer possible. I'm so lonely I could cry. Woe is me. But it's comforting to know I'm not the only one who feels this way."

I know Aristotle said art was about pity, but he didn't mean self-pity. Pity is not a viable artistic relation to your characters—just like it's not a viable relation to real people in life or to yourself. It's patronizing. Adolescent. Sentimental. Real art is never about pity—or self-pity.

LaBute is another story. At least Paul Thomas Anderson and Todd Solondz seem sincere. LaBute is calculating, cynical, and manipulative. Think of Laclos's *Les Liasons Dangereuses* or Da Ponte's *Cosi fan Tutte*—without Mozart's music, of course. Films like *Your Friends and Neighbors* and *In the Company of Men* rely on shock-tactics. They play with narrative expectations, reverse things, and trick the viewer. But you can't create great art out of shock effects and surprises. Shock grabs your attention but doesn't reward it. Narratively, LaBute is as cold-blooded and as out-of-touch with the complexities of actual lived experience as his main characters are.

In short, you haven't really escaped something if you have to keep putting it down or regretting that things aren't the way Hollywood movies say they are. The goal should be to break free of the stupidity of Hollywood ways of understanding, not keep being upset by the fact that life isn't the way Hollywood movies say it is.

Friedman: How does a filmmaker do that?

Carney: Grow up. Get over it. Leave the heroes and villains behind. Leave the romantic myths behind. Capture a reality that doesn't have good or bad, angels or devils. Depict a world that isn't organized around swoony-moony Hollywood love and heroism, but that does not leave you disillusioned and despairing by that fact. Move your work beyond both idealism and cynicism. That is the place of truth. The challenge of art is no different from the challenge of life: to embrace the truth, the whole truth, and nothing but the truth.

The Poetry of What Is

Friedman: How can that be done?

Carney: Look at *Ghost World*. It's one of the best films of the last ten years. Terry Zwigoff not only creates a movie without Hollywood visionary depths and melodramatic intensities, but one that doesn't nostalgically long for such things and regret their unavailability. He creates a world without spiritual peaks and valleys, without wild romantic passions, without sentimental mood music orchestrations or tight close-ups. But he doesn't get into a funk about it. He accepts it. In effect, he says, that's life. Deal with it. He and his characters accept what is and what isn't and go on from there. His characters are flawed and flat and weak, but rather than condemning them for not being white horse heroes, the way Solondz or Paul Thomas Anderson would, Zwigoff appreciates them. What's the Robert Frost line? He loves them for what they are. *Ghost World* leaves Hollywood behind without looking back. Zwigoff is not nostalgic for heroes and sentiment and ideals. He accepts and affirms rather than regrets and bemoans. The earth is as flat as a cartoon; but so what? Now that we know that, we can still go somewhere.

Caveh Zahedi does something just as interesting in *A Little Stiff*. He captures the clumsiness, the embarrassments, the disappointments of life. Zahedi is a little like Wes Anderson, but better than Anderson because he doesn't take the easy way out and "play cute." Andrew Bujalski does it in *Mutual Appreciation*. He creates a world as socially complex and emotionally layered as Renoir's *Rules of the Game,* and as lacking in visionary releases and romantic expansions. The characters don't have the option of imaginatively enlarging themselves in the Hollywood way. They have to just muddle through. David Barker creates a totally different but equally fascinating non-melodramatic world in *Afraid of Everything*. And Vince Gallo does something different from all of them and just as unsentimental in *Buffalo 66*. Up until the sentimental ending, at least.

Friedman: *Can you say more about Wes Anderson's work?*

Carney: I'll give him his due. He lets his actors act. An actor's performance can bring out a lot of complex feelings that the words in a script never get near. So the performance part of his work is a plus. So many other movies don't have any acting in them at all to speak of. Just people playing scenes, reading lines.

But Anderson's films are hobbled by two limitations. First, as I already said, they are suffused with nostalgia for some golden age when everybody lived in one big happy family. It's an adolescent belief. There never was, there never could be, such a time. He and his characters are locked in states of arrested development. Like they never got over their pre-teen years. During *Royal Tenenbaums*, I wanted to yell at the screen: "Enough already about not being loved, Wes. Enough about dysfunctional families. Enough about how much fun it was when you and your friends could all hang out together. Let your characters grow up. Let them let go of the past. Let them get over their childhood lack of love. Or their parents' divorce. There's life after high school. Make a movie about that."

Nostalgia for a past that never was is part of the romantic myth I already talked about. Nostalgia is a young person's version of history. When you're twenty, five or ten years ago seems like the middle ages. It's a button you can push to get a guaranteed emotion from a person of a certain age, but that doesn't change the fact that it's an avoidance of getting on with your life here and now. A thousand years from now, people will study these movies as pathology. They tell us a lot about the infantilization of our culture.

The second limitation of Anderson's work is that he is afraid of upsetting his audience. He turns things into jokes too much. His sense of humor gets the better of him. It allows him to take the easy way out of difficult scenes. I heard him say in an interview that someday he'd like to make a movie that didn't have a joke in it. Well so would I. I'd like to see him avoid using Owen Wilson's goof-ball clowning-around or Bill Murray's charming hammi-ness to get out of a sticky situation. Anderson lets his actors act, but he apparently doesn't detect that they are using cuteness to avoid having actually to reveal anything. But again Anderson didn't invent that problem either. Terminal cuteness is another curse of our culture. Look at how tal-ents like Jack Nicholson, Nick Cage, Chris Walken, and Robert DeNiro have squandered enormous chunks of their careers by mugging their way through roles. Enough with "The Joker."

But can I go back to the question of what can be done positively? Let me make clear that I don't want young directors to go off and re-make *Ghost World* or *Little Stiff*. You don't have to do it those ways. Express your own vision. The world may be flat, and our personalities may be messed-up and confused, but every artist finds a new path through life's disappointments and struggles. And there are a lot of them—and not only when you're young!

Great art gives a jillion illustrations of how you can embrace realities—giv-ing up what is not, while still being able to rejoice in what is. Listen to Bach's *St. Matthew Passion*. Look at Rembrandt's portraits. Read Chekhov's plays or Alice Munro's stories. In their different ways, they all tell us that the toughness of life, the disappointments, the weirdness is inseparable from its beauty. If you screen out the hard realities, you deny life. I saw a quote from Chekhov a couple weeks ago that sums it up. He said the most beautiful landscape has cow manure in it—and in fact was created by the cow manure—that bad, selfish, destructive emotions are as much a part of the meaning of life as noble, idealistic ones. To leave out the cow manure and the venality is to reject life. Chekhov doesn't put pettiness and fear into his plays to do dirt on life, to undermine his characters in the LaBute way, but to tell the whole truth about experience—about how interesting, complex, mysterious it is. You have to find a way to love life without deny-ing its imperfections. You have to find a way to love the imperfections! That's what Frans Hals did. That's what Lenny Bruce and Richard Pryor and Bill Hicks did. That's what Renoir and Cassavetes and May did, and what Kiarostami and Leigh and Von Trier still do. The important point is that the greatest works of art, like the greatest moments in our lives, are always acts of reverence and love and respect. They show the pettiness and flaws but still affirm the wonder. They don't regret what isn't; they celebrate what is. They bless rather than curse. And they don't ask us to feel sorry for ourselves or retreat into some past that never was.

Innocence and Idealism

Friedman: Some media/cultural critics talk about sentimentality as a by-product of an industrial society unable to feel without "emotional guide-posts." Like we have to be told where to take pictures at Disneyland!

Carney: Look, we live in a consumer culture. Americans are consumers. Trained from birth to buy, buy, buy to fill their spiritual void—like the little girl I saw in the supermarket the other day pushing a tiny cart with a flag on it that read "shopper in training." It's kind of cute when they're two, but it gets spooky when they turn twenty-two and define themselves in terms of the shoes and jeans and jackets they buy.

Our culture trains people in consumption, with objects just being the tip of the iceberg. The trivial part is buying things—cars, clothing, computers; the important part is buying values and emotions. We are trained from birth to mimic, to imitate, to take our feelings, ideas, beliefs, and meanings from outside ourselves. When you do that long enough you forget what you really need and want and feel.

If Americans can buy invading a country, toppling its government, and unleashing civil war as being a noble, heroic act, it's clear that they'll buy just about anything as long as it is marketed in the right way—with a designer label, a sentimental story, or, in the case of Iraq and a lot else, an appeal to their ideals.

Ideals and sentimental stories are terrific marketing devices. Benneton and Nike showed that years ago in terms of objects, but TV shows and movies and the evening news have been doing it decades longer with values. Hollywood is the greatest marketer of ideals in the history of the world. They're selling and Americans by the millions are buying. Look at the popularity of *Titanic* and *The Matrix* and *Shrek* and *Lord of the Rings* and *Harry Potter.*

Friedman: Why do you think those films were so popular?

Carney: Because America is the most idealistic culture that ever existed in the history of the world. It was founded on dreams of democratic decision-making, individual rights, personal fulfillment, and free expression. And these films present ideal, idealized visions of life and personal expression. Totally American and totally phony, superficial, stupid.

Don't get me wrong. There is nothing wrong with the ideals themselves. I believe in them myself. What I object to is the fact that they have been hijacked by marketers, corporations, government leaders, and filmmakers to sell us things—and have been dumbed down in the process. They have been co-opted by corporations and government officials to serve unidealistic ends. They have been turned into slogans and marketing strategies to pursue cynical, manipulative, selfish purposes. That's the story of Hollywood filmmaking. But that's trivial of course. It's also why we are in Iraq. It's why such stupid people get elected year after year. It's why Americans don't see what their culture is really doing abroad. In being turned into marketing ploys, complex ideals have been translated into children's bedtime stories. They have been disconnected from reality. American foreign policy becomes a series of emotions unrelated to facts, feelings without knowledge. As I said before, that's my definition of sentimentality. The sentimentality of our movies is the least of our worries. The sentimentality of our culture is absolutely terrifying.

Friedman: Why don't people see what is being done?

Carney: Because America is a naïve, innocent, childlike culture. That little girl with the shopping cart is us. We are being manipulated. And we love it. We want to be turned into shoppers. We want to be told what to think and how to feel. We want the easy version of experience.

Friedman: I don't follow.

Carney: The ideals America was founded on, and is, at least in theory, still devoted to, represent complex contracts with experience. They put challenges to us. They make demands on us. They ask us to do difficult things. When they are turned into marketing slogans and bedtime stories—in the movies, on the evening news, in American politics—they suddenly become simple and easy and painless. Even a war can be painless if someone else is sent to fight it. Because of the immaturity of our culture—the shallowness of our educational system, the demagoguery of our politics, the cravenness of our media—people accept the fairy-tale version of the ideal.

Consider freedom. It can't simply be given to someone. We are not born free. We have to achieve it. We have to struggle for it—against a thousand alien entanglements. We are up to our eyeballs in clichés, conventions, received ideas, provincialisms, bumper-sticker substitutes for thought. It's hard to break free of all that. And it takes more than effort and will-power. It takes intelligence, knowledge, sensitivity, awareness. You can't just will yourself free. That's what most Americans don't seem to understand and the political and corporate marketers have no intention of telling them. Americans want the easy, know-nothing path to emotional and intellectual freedom. "Tell me who to be. Tell me what to think. Tell me how to feel. Tell me what to buy." That's the context within which the Hollywood selling of meanings and emotions and the public's willingness to buy them has to be understood.

The mistake is to look to movies for any answers at all. All movies can really do is point out problems, pose questions, set us tasks to do. They can remind us that we need to work on our lives. They can ask us to open our consciousnesses to new ways of knowing and feeling. They can inspire us to try harder. But they can't give us answers. They can't do the work for us. We have to do it all. Nothing can lift that burden from our shoulders. And that takes time and work and thought. It's not quick and painless. People don't want that kind of movie. That's an art film! [Laughs].They want to pay their ten dollars and get ten conventional, predictable emotions in exchange, and if possible an answer or two about how to live their lives.

Anyone who wants anything else to give him or her values is in big trouble. You can't buy them or buy into them or you become just another consumer. You are just asking to be sold a bill of goods.

Make no mistake about it: there are thousands of emotional snake-oil salesmen just waiting to sell you cheap, shoddy, knock-offs of American ideals and values. [Like a carnival barker:] "Step right up, ladies and gentlemen. The line forms on the left. In the front we have William Kristol, Richard Perle, and Karl Rove, leaning against each. On the right there's Jack Welch and Rupert Murdoch and Bill O'Reilly and the McLaughlin Group shouting at each other. Charlie Rose is next to them, smiling at how entertaining it is. And for the ladies, in the row right behind them, we have Steven Spielberg, Diane Sawyer, Barbara Walters, Oprah Winfrey, Oliver Stone, Dr. Phil, Ron Howard, and Tom Hanks holding hands and speaking quietly and sincerely."

But, listen, I can't talk about this any more. It's too sad, too depressing.

America could be so great and the world could be such a different place if we lived up to the ideals that we profess to believe in. We could be doing really wonderful things to end poverty and hunger and slaughter and demagoguery and we're not. We're only making things worse. It hurts to think about all the missed opportunities year after year, decade after decade. I believe in Emerson, but I'm afraid Tocqueville may have been closer to the truth.

Anyway, I've already written so much about this desire to look to movies and television as sources of value that anyone interested should just read my Capra or my Dreyer or my Leigh or my *What's Wrong... and How to Do it Right* book or something else I've written.

Manufactured Emotions

Friedman: What to you distinguishes genuine emotion in art from fake emotion, i.e., genuine human empathy from manipulated sentimentality? How do we get back to the genuine in film—free from guideposts? Isn't all film a manipulation? Isn't any emotion real?

Carney: You want me to tell you how to tell a fake emotion from real one? You should be asking Charlotte Beck, not me. She's a Zen Master who's written books about the subject. Beautiful books. I'm not as smart as she is, but I'll take a stab at an answer by saying something that may sound weird. As far as I am concerned, ninety-nine percent of all of the emotions we experience both in life and in Hollywood movies are what you are calling—and what I am calling—"fake." Our culture is a machine for creating plastic feelings—a panoply of petty, personal, egoistic conflicts, needs, and demands: our obsession with possessions and appearances—from houses to cars to clothing; our need to keep up with the latest gadgets, trends, news, and events; our concerns about glamour and charm and what other people think of us; our feeling that we need to fight, struggle, and compete to get ahead—and a million other self-destructive fears and insecurities. They are everywhere. And they are all unreal. Made up. Crazy. Cuckoo. Destructive of what we really are and need and feel.

We put ourselves on an emotional hamster track we can never get to the end of. And we love the whole insane rat-race! The push and pull of the bustling, grabbing, self-centered ego has become our substitute for the soul, which we let peek out a few times a year at church or synagogue or when we listen to classical music. Our desire to be "entertained" by a movie or that it have high drama or a thrilling plot is part of the same shallow, meaningless, endless quest for synthetic excitement, glamour, stimulation. Bad art is organized around the same titillating, animalistic emotions as bad living. There are valuable, good, real emotions—truer, deeper, more authentic ways of being and feeling and knowing—but the problem with Hollywood and television and newspapers and the rest of the media is that they are devoted to presenting, manipulating, and exalting the self-destructive, self-centered, artificial, trivial feelings. In fact, as far as I can tell, movies and experiences organized around ego-centered emotions are the ones people love the most. Just like they love football games more than they love ballet. It's because the fake emotions plug into our reptilian brain stems and are reinforced by a whole cultural system of programming.

Bad art is a vast emotional recycling operation. It recycles pre-existing, mass-produced, artificial feelings already out there in the culture. Good art creates entirely new and different feelings—original, unexpected, surprising ones. If that is hard to understand, all I can say is that my Leigh book has more than you want to know about this subject. It's also what I was trying to explain in my Cassavetes books when I argued that his work—like all great art—asks us to think and feel in fresh ways. Nothing is prefabricated or plastic. But I've discovered it is a hard concept to get across. When I call the feelings in other films fake, my students get confused. They say people really feel these emotions. Their pulses really beat faster during the ending of *The Matrix*. They really cry at the end of *Titanic*. They really care who wins in *Erin Brockovich*. They really feel elated when a villain gets blown up in the *Star Wars* movies. In life, people really get choked up when they put an American flag in front of their house or a yellow ribbon on their car. And my students are right. To the people who experience these feelings, they are real. But that doesn't mean they aren't fake. Maybe it would be better to call them mental emotions, since they are created by our thoughts. They are in our heads. That's what's wrong with them. They represent postures, stances, and attitudes that make us feel good about ourselves. Even as we torture ourselves by casting ourselves in this endless, draining struggle, these emotions flatter us because they inflate our importance. We struggle so we can feel we are getting ahead. We keep up with the Joneses so we can feel superior to them. Even as it hurts them, people love to create self-justifying emotional dramas this way.

Bad movies play on our emotional weaknesses, but great ones can move us beyond these clichés or show us their limitations. But you can't look to

Hollywood for that kind of movie. Look at Bresson's *Lancelot* or *Femme Douce*. Look at Dreyer's *Day of Wrath* or *Gertrud*. Or look at Cassavetes' *Faces*, Leigh's *Abigail's Party*, Rappaport's *Local Color,* or Noonan's *The Wife*—four absolutely brilliant, extended dissections of the emotional unreality we imprison ourselves within. These films reveal how pervasive and self-destructive fake feelings are.

The Seductions of Stylishness

Friedman: Sometimes it seems like even so-called art films many times gloss over the interior life of their characters and become rather cynical reflections of the filmmakers' unwillingness to grapple with deep questions. Why do you think this is?

Carney: I agree. Of course, cynicism never goes by its own name. It is always called something else: smartness, stylishness, coolness, playfulness, wit. Look at *L.A. Confidential*. David Denby called it one of the best films of the decade. Or *Pulp Fiction,* which every critic in America had multiple orgasms over. Or the complete work of John Dahl or the Coen brothers. Highbrow critics absolutely love hard, mechanical film noir. The quantity of inner life, the truth, the depth of the experience in the film never enters into their calculations. In fact the more cynical, manipulative, and tough the movie—the more heartlessly witty and hard-edged it is—the more they like it.

Friedman: Why do you think that is?

Carney: Well, for Denby and Anthony Lane and other self-styled "intellectual" journalists, it's a reaction against all the smarmy, sentimental gush that they have to sit through every other day of their lives. It's what they feel sets them apart from the sappy, stupid, Leonard Maltin/Gene Shalit-type critics who like *Titanic* or *Pearl Harbor*. To be wised-up, cynical, and "smart" in this way is their definition of what it is to be an intellectual. It's a high-school definition, but they don't realize it.

These films are as much about flattering the viewer as Hollywood movies are, but it's just a different kind of viewer. These critics can feel intelligent because they get the cinematic in-jokes. They can feel clever because they appreciate the narrative or visual cleverness. The more the whole experience has a patina of Penn and Teller knowingness and cynicism to it—you know, "Hey, it's all stupid, but watch me pull another friggin' stupid rabbit out of a friggin' stupid hat"—the more they like it. They think these movies reveal how manipulative other movies are. They think they reveal how everybody who falls for the sentiment in other movies is a donkey. Everybody but them! They and the filmmaker are insiders. Hey, lighten up, it's all just hocus-pocus-dominocus.

There's also a gender component to it. It's no accident that most of these critics—and the filmmakers they adore—are men. It's a boy thing. A teenage boy thing. "Look at how tough I am. How unsentimental I can be. I'm a real guy." The same critics who canonized Lynch in the 1980s and Tarantino in the 1990s loved those half-jokesy, glossy, ironic horror films by Tobe Hooper, John Carpenter, and Brian De Palma in the seventies. Twenty years later, they still haven't grown up.

Look at *Mulholland Drive*. And, for an even more depressing experience, look at the critical accolades showered on it. *Film Comment* devoted a large part of an entire issue to it. In celebration of what? A series of smart-ass tricks and games. Big friggin' deal. That's the best someone can do with a couple million dollars? I don't care how the New York critics revel in it, or what they call it, it's cynicism to me. You wouldn't need all the emotional back-flips and narrative trap doors if you had anything to say. You wouldn't need doppelgangers and shadow-figures if your characters had souls. I always think of something Robert Frost's students said he used to ask over and over again in class: "Is this poem sincere?" Robert Graves had a similar bullshit test. He used to ask, "Is this poem necessary?" Those are not bad questions to ask about any work of art. Movies like *Mulholland Drive* and *Kill Bill* are not about sincerity or necessity but stylishness. We don't learn anything important about life from them.

The adoration of cleverness, the love of wit isn't something new. Lynch's fan club didn't invent this value system. Oscar Wilde was prancing down this runway a long time ago. The critics loved it then and they love it now. Look at the votive lights that have been tended at the Hitchcock shrine for more than fifty years. I was leafing through an old issue of *MovieMaker* where a good friend of mine, David Sterritt, was being interviewed and described Hitchcock as a "philosopher-poet." That got my attention. That's what a filmmaker should be. So I couldn't wait to read his answer to the next question the interviewer asked—about what made Hitchcock's work so great? I was all set for a poetic, philosophical answer. Then Sterritt said something about the way in *Psycho* the first thing visible in Sam and

Marion's hotel room is the "bathroom" and the way the driving in the rain scene involved "water and blades." Get it? Marion is killed in a bathroom, in the shower, with water streaming down her body, by a blade, and—ta dah!—there are all these allusions to bathrooms, showers, and blades earlier in the film. Can you run that by me again? Is that the poetry part or the philosophy part?

It's an immature notion of art. I can understand the appeal. Everyone went through that stage. I did too. In high school. The class read *The Great Gatsby* and when we were done, the teacher pointed out these metaphors. The green light and all those other references. I thought I had understood the novel before that. But then I suddenly realized how I had missed all this metaphoric stuff. I raced though the text finding all these things I hadn't realized were there. It was like reading a different book. It was a heady experience. It was exciting. I had never known you could do that. There was all this hidden stuff, just waiting to be excavated. That must be what a work of art is. It had secret meanings. Wow. Amazing. I felt like an intellectual for the first time when I did it. But that was high school for gosh sake. I was just a kid. I got over it. A few years later, sometime in college I guess, I realized how trivial it all was. That it was all just a parlor trick. But there are apparently thousands of film reviewers and students and professors out there who never got over the green light at the end of *Gatsby*. Art is about finding hidden messages in invisible bottles thrown ashore by the artist. It's that pattern that emerges when you connect the dots. Bathroom. Rain. Wiper blades. Shower scene. Knife blade. Get it? It's all so clear. So crisp. So abstract. So tempting. It's the pleasure of filling out a crossword puzzle or manipulating one of those cereal box decoder rings and cracking the code. "Look at what I can do. Look at the secret connections I can find." It's pretty intoxicating. Like finding the word that slips magically into 12 down and links with 5 and 7 across. It gives the critic all this power over the text. It makes him feel smart.

Clear Mysteries

The only problem is that that's not what you do to art or what real art does to you. When you watch a Cassavetes or Noonan movie, even for the tenth time, you are not doing a crossword puzzle. You are not playing connect the dots. You are not turning over stones looking for sermons underneath them. The meanings are not hidden in that way and they are not revealed or decoded in that way. Oh, there are probably people who try to do this to

Cassavetes—just as they try to do it to Rembrandt and Balanchine—but that doesn't make it right. The meanings in his works aren't those kinds of meanings. They don't snap into place with a satisfying click. The computer programmers talk about "fuzzy logic." Well, Noonan's and Cassavetes' and Leigh's and Rembrandt's meanings are murky, fuzzy meanings. I was just teaching Mike Leigh's *Meantime* in class yesterday. I was trying to show the students how the film is a triumph of not spelling things out, not pinning them down, not clarifying its meanings. Leigh gets us to the same place life at its best does. The effect is extraordinary. And so different from Hollywood. In the Renaissance, they called this "sfumato," smoky meaning. That's not something against it. That's what is great about it. The meaning is not clear and distinct like an idea, but fuzzy like an experience. You don't "get" it like a *New Yorker* cartoon. You undergo it; you live with it; you live into it. It's the difference between mysteries and acts of mystification, between the real complexity of life and the bogus fakery of bad art.

I talk about this at length in my Leigh book and my Cambridge Cassavetes book. At one point in the Cassavetes book I contrast the kinds of meanings made by *The Killing of a Chinese Bookie* and *Citizen Kane*. Cassavetes' movie makes unclear, partial, hesitant, tentative meanings. Welles's makes sharp, clear, distinct ones. When the smoke goes up the chimney at the end of Kane it is the opposite of a smoky meaning. It's as clear as a bell. Of course that's why people love Kane. They have the fun of "getting it" loud and clear.

Art as Ideas Versus Art as Experiences

Friedman: Is the clarity of the meanings why people enjoy films like these?

Carney: People would rather play games, do crossword puzzles, watch tricks than face reality and deal with hard questions. It's a form of intellectual escapism. Decoding puzzle-films are a way of flattering themselves that they are smart and hip and "with-it." These movies are for teenagers who are too young to understand much about life or for adults too intimidated by the complexity of adult life to want to grapple with it.

Appreciating great art is totally different from doing a crossword puzzle. My pal David Sterritt should not be asking what he can do to Hitchcock, but what Hitchcock can do to and for him. Ultimately, it all comes down to how much the work can show us about life—the density and complexity and flow of reality that it captures and exposes us to. Reading Joyce Carol Oates and Alice Munro and Eudora Welty is like living life on steroids, on speed, on hyperdrive. Let me emphasize what I just said: not reading about life, but living it. I have experiences like the ones I have in life—just as slippery and elusive and changeable—but even more interesting than the ones life usually provides, because they come at me faster, and they are richer, more complex, and more demanding than those in my everyday life. Hack your way through Oates's "Missing Person," "Goose Girl," and "American, Abroad" if you want to see what I mean. I happen to be teaching all three of them this week. They are like doing emotional rock-climbing. You build new emotional muscles, you stretch yourself in new directions, you feel new things, as you gingerly pick a path through them, word by word, sentence by sentence. My *What's Wrong... and How to Do it Right* book is all about this sense of art.

David Sterritt should ask what *Psycho* can show him about his desires and needs, his relationship to his lover, his family, his life. The answer would be: very little. And that, if you want to know, is why Hitchcock is not a great artist but an entertainer with just enough cleverness and panache and visual dazzle to impress the pseudo-intellectuals. His works are kitsch. Fake art. Pretend art.

Friedman: Is there a reason filmmakers are making so many movies with visual games and narrative surprises? Movies like Being John Malkovich, Adaptation, and Run, Lola, Run?

Carney: There are dozens of these films and they are some of the most influential movies among my students. In addition to the ones you've named, I'd add *Memento, Suture, Waking Life, The Truman Show,* and *Eternal Sunshine of the Spotless Mind. The Matrix* also falls into this category. Oh, I just thought of some more. There are so many. But to answer your question, I'm of two minds about the popularity of these works.

On the one hand, I know that many young people go to these movies out of a sincere desire to have a deeper and more thoughtful experience than they can get in an ordinary dramatic film. They want to grapple with questions about the ultimate nature of reality and our place in it, about how the world's systems of understanding are organized, about "what it all means." For that kind of viewer these movies provide a cosmic, panoramic, intellectual experience. Watching them is less like watching a normal movie than going to church or reading philosophy.

Although films like *Magnolia* and *American Beauty* and *Boogie Nights* are different in some ways, that sense of enlarging your perspective, of actually learning things, things that you don't learn in a regular movie is a large part of their appeal too. Because of the size of their casts and the generational scope of their stories, young people feel that they are getting a larger, deeper, more comprehensive vision of the world than the one in a Hollywood movie. They have the feeling that these movies give them an inside view of the world of adult life, a view of hidden realities that they otherwise don't have access to. Watching these movies feels like being able to hear what your parents talk about when their bedroom door is closed. Watching them feels like having the secrets of adulthood revealed to you.

Now I can understand and sympathize with both kinds of appeal. When I was young, the only difference was that I went to books as much as to films to try to break the codes of the world. For sociology, I read Paul Goodman and Vance Packard and Alfred Kinsey and David Reisman and the Hite Report. For philosophy, I read Ayn Rand, Herman Hesse, Carlos Castenada, Alan Watts, Nietzsche, and Lin Yutang. [Laughs] I know, I know. I was young! It's a totally embarrassing list! I sat through *My Dinner with André* to get the same philosophical rush I did from the books. And I watched *The Graduate* and *Who's Afraid of Virginia Woolf* to see what adults did after I went to bed, what they really thought and felt and said when kids weren't around.

Superficial Profundity and Profound Superficiality

But at some point you leave those understandings behind. What's the bible verse? "When I was a child I saw as a child, but now I am a man and I see as a man." Well ... something like that! [Laughs] At some point you learn that the strangeness of the human heart can be more surprising and less predictable than all of quantum theory. In a word, you realize that experiences can be much more complex and interesting than ideas.

At that point you realize that Spike Jonze's mysticism for the millions is just a lot of eyewash. You realize that *Magnolia*'s vision of adulthood as a repository of dirty secrets is a superficial way to understand adult life. You realize that Anderson's invocation of suppressed depths, his obsession with revelations and breakdowns, are just cheap ways of attaching drama and interest to otherwise fairly shallow, boring characters and situations. All of his major characters are wearing masks, hiding dark secrets. That seems revelatory when you are 18, but it's a high-school notion of depth, a child's understanding of what it is to be an adult.

David Lynch's and the Coen brothers' work is no deeper. I blame it on Hitchcock. And all those critics who force-fed his work to generations of undergraduates. And Welles. It's the lamentable legacy of all of those critical paeans to *Citizen Kane*—the fallacy of thinking that truth is in the depths, when it's really on the surface. It's not the things adults hide that matter; it's the things they show. The great mystery of life is not the invisible, but the visible. What makes us fascinating is not what we don't say, but what we do. But it takes a while to realize that.

Films like *What Happened Was* and *Faces* and *Mikey and Nicky* and *Wanda* make the work of Jonze and Anderson and Solondz and Lynch look like *Sesame Street*. They don't rely on shock tactics and surprise revelations. They don't need special effects, narrative tricks, or revelations to make things dramatic. The characters don't have to have deep, dark secrets in order to hold our interest.

The salesmen in *Faces* are fascinating not because of what they hide from us, but because of what they show us. There is no mask to remove, no hidden truth to unveil. What makes them interesting is not what they aren't, but what they are. Cassavetes' characters are mysterious because they don't have any mysteries. They are deep because everything you need to know about them is on the surface. If they had secrets they would be easier to understand. In our love of depths, we've forgotten that the surface is the most complex place there is.

This search for secrets is just another version of the "decoder ring" understanding of experience. My real fear is that, culturally speaking, we are losing extraordinarily valuable forms of understanding.

Losing Consciousness

Friedman: What does that mean? How can you lose a way of understanding?

Carney: It's a real danger. Young people in the current generation have intellectually been worked over for so long and to such an extent that they are in real danger of losing the awareness that there can be anything deeper than these shallow versions of profundity. There are dozens of cultural forces and factions working to limit their consciousnesses: from the multicultural ideologues who teach them to measure things in sociological terms, to the allegorists who want them to translate their experiences into abstractions, to the pop-culture slumlords who want to deny them their intellectual and artistic heritage by ignoring or downplaying the high culture masterworks—the greatest achievements of the human heart and mind.

All of the interesting aspects of art, all the things that make art drop out of the analysis: style, tone, and performance among other things. I just read a thesis proposal on Vladimir Nabokov's *Lolita* from a student who apparently has never grappled with the idea that style can bend or color the content of a work. She treated the novel like it was a story in the newspaper. Nabokov was writing about a dirty old man molesting an innocent pre-teen. And she, of course, was interested in writing about the cultural history of men who exploit women. I thought of the Robert Frost quote that "poetry is what is lost in the translation." Well, the novel was what was lost in her translation of it into sociology. I wish she were an exception. I just read a set of papers about *Buffalo 66* that did the same thing. The weirdness, the extravagance, the pushiness, the insecurity, the swagger of the film's style disappeared. It became a boy-meets-girl love story. When I have students read Stanley Elkin or look at Mark Rappaport movies, they do the same thing. They treat the works like they were equivalent to the events in them, and talk about the characters like they were real people. Estelle should get a life, and Bernie Perk, he sure is a weird druggist. They can't deal with the stylization. They blow right by it. They read right through it. But the style is the reason the work exists.

Reminds me of two essays I got in a literature course when I was first starting out at Middlebury. Both from the same student. The first was about "moody, broody Hamlet, who missed his dad so much." The second was about "poor, old, neglected, unloved King Lear." Like Hamlet was a boyfriend who should go to the college counseling services and get some help, and Lear was some lonely old guy who lived down the street! I guess she could next do Othello as a victim of racism. That's not what Jan Kott meant when he called Shakespeare "our contemporary"! [Laughs] That's not why we read the plays.

It would be funny if it weren't so sad. The contemporary psychological and sociological steamroller levels everything in its path. The style gets flattened. The Shakespeare in the play disappears. We see how ridiculous it is to do this to *Lear* and *Hamlet*—at least I hope we do!—but we seem to think it's OK to do it with a lot of film. Must be the seductions of photographic realism. Anyway, that's what I mean by saying these students are being denied their intellectual heritage by a *60 Minutes/20-20/Dateline* approach to art. It's a terrible loss.

You can lose a whole way of understanding in a single generation. Scientists and mathematicians realize that. They know that if you discontinue research in a certain area of knowledge, you can cut off progress in it for the next century. Musicians know it. How many people beyond musicians still understand the nuances of something as basic as sonata-allegro form? What every well-educated person in 1791 Vienna "spoke" has become a lost language. English professors, at least ones in the older generation, understand that you can lose ways of reading, forms of linguistic awareness and sensitivity. Well, in film study, we're in danger of losing delicate, subtle ways of understanding film. They are being replaced by simpler, cruder forms of knowing—Marxist, feminist, psychological, sociological, metaphorical, symbolic, and dozens of other mechanical, preformulated forms of understanding.

You want another example? Most of my grad students can't understand meanings that won't stand still. They try to nail everything down. [Laughs] D.H. Lawrence calls it nailing Christ to the cross. And most of them can't understand meanings that resist clarifying themselves—meanings that are bent and colored and inflected by tones and moods. All their training has programmed them to deal with meanings that don't shift and change, meanings that are flat and simple and monotonic and "on the nose." All their classroom experiences have been devoted to treating meaning as something abstract and atemporal. They have lost the ability to deal with fluid, flexible, multivalent, unresolved forms of experience.
Well, that's what I am talking about. Those are enormous cultural losses. Tragic losses—of inestimably important ways of thinking and feeling.

Friedman: Why do you think the students are getting worse?

Carney: Well, I wasn't actually arguing that the students are getting worse. The Middlebury example shows that literalism has been around for a long time. What is getting worse is the teaching. It's the teachers who are the problem. The students just do what they are taught to do. In the past professors who taught arts—fiction, dance, drama, poetry, etc.—used to root out this naïve realism and move students beyond it, but now as far as I can tell, they encourage it, because it plugs into so many contemporary ideological projects—like reading texts as honoring multicultural diversity and "otherness." A racial reading of *Othello* not only wouldn't be laughed at today, but probably encouraged. The student would then be told to do a feminist reading of Othello's relationship to Desdemona.

But, you know, maybe teaching hasn't really changed that much. Leon Edel's writing on Henry James, Richard Ellman's on James Joyce, and A.C. Bradley's on Shakespeare show that even a long time ago big name academics were unable to read great literature. There have always been flat-minded readings and weak readers among both students and professors. There is no reason to wax nostalgic that earlier generations of teachers and students were great at dealing with the subtleties of style and tone.

Style and tone are hard to grapple with. They always have been and always will be. We are always more comfortable with clarity and literalism than ulteriority and indirection and inflection and grace notes and "bending." The fluidity of temporal experience always presents a challenge—in art and life. The shift and flow of meaning in a complex work of art is always going to test our capacities of responsiveness. We're not good at dealing with change, indeterminacy, and in-betweenness.

It relates to our evolutionary past, to how our brains have been wired to process information. We are much better and more comfortable dealing with stasis. Our brains are tuned to grapple with objects rather than experiences, with fixities rather than fluidities. We conceptualize life in terms of adjectives and nouns rather than verbs and adverbs. Our brains have been programmed to freeze experience into ideas, conclusions, predictions. We sort, arrange, and categorize—we close down cognitively—we should stay open and responsive to the flow of experience. That's just the way the mind works. It has a certain amount of survival value, which is why evolution has bred it into us, but it gets us into a lot of trouble in the rest of life, especially in complex social experiences; but that part of us won't change until evolution changes it. Or until some Zen Master comes along and helps us see our rigidities.

And there's a kind of evolutionary reward system at work in the classroom too. My argument is that the current generation of students has been rewarded for their mistakes—rather than being told they are wrong— because of the influence of all of the sociological understandings they have had thrust at them by the media and by their teachers. And, at the opposite extreme, films like *The Matrix* and *Pulp Fiction* and the glitziness of MTV visuals have desensitized them to the sheer strangeness of style. The result is a particularly pervasive and damaging 21st-century form of critical flat-mindedness.

Safe Danger

Friedman: So many films are more like roller-coaster rides of stimulation rather than windows into human experience.

Carney: That's true. People love to be taken on an amusement park ride. You know why? Because the danger is fake. There are a few thrills and chills, but they don't last long and you always end up back in the light. It's not really demanding and confusing. You don't need to worry because it's not really like life. It's safe danger—like a game. People want that. They want simple, manageable emotions. They want easy, predictable, controllable excitement. Don't spoil my date. Don't make me ask real questions about my life. Hey, lighten up, will ya? The best of Bresson's, Rossellini's, De Sica's, Ozu's, Cassavetes' work gets our emotions to places that aren't manageable in this way. We can't walk away laughing.

Friedman: But you are forgetting that people respond strongly to Hollywood films.

Carney: Yeah, and they get worked up over the Super Bowl too. That doesn't make it art. In my film classes, I sometimes do a unit on ballet and modern dance to show students the expressive power of gesture and movement, and some of my boy grad students—with great sincerity and conviction mind you—tell me that they don't get much out of the modern dance or ballet tapes, but they "know what I mean," since they feel "the exact same things someone at the ballet does" when they watch a linebacker or tackle scramble in a football game. I have the embarrassing job of informing them that, no, they don't understand what I am trying to show them. Lawrence Taylor was not doing the same thing as Paul Taylor.

The issue of whether you feel something or not is not a sufficient test of the value of a work. Our feelings are too primitive. Too easily elicited. I can get excited by the final minute of a Final Four playoff game. But I don't mistake it for a work of art. Art is less about feeling than seeing, thinking, and understanding in new ways. Less about emotion than knowledge. The cry of a baby can make me feel sad, but it's not a work of art. Burt Bachrach may bring a tear to your eye, but that doesn't make him Bach.

I tell the boys who want to equate Michael Jordan with Suzanne Farrell, that they have to ask what they learn from the experience of watching Michael Jordan. Does it change or enrich their understanding of the rest of life? Or does it just play into their pre-existing emotional clichés? Does it leave them thoughtful and deeper or just breathless and excited? If they want that, you're right, they might as well go on a roller-coaster ride. Great art is not about revving us up. That's what a sales conference or How-to-Make-a-Fortune-in-Real-Estate seminar is for. The greatest art is more likely to take us through an experience that humbles and abashes us— that chastens, bewilders, and hushes us into silence at what we suddenly realize we have failed to see and experience up until then. That's pretty different from a video game or a roller-coaster ride.

As you said before and your roller-coaster comparison implies, these films lack complex, interesting, adult inner life. The only inner life most popular movies have is defined by thrills and chills, suspense, fear, or mystification. That tells us everything we need to know about them. What kind of inner world is that? It's the inner world of a shark. A dog, a horse, a baboon has a more complex consciousness than that.

Inner life is everything. What else is there? The rest is capitalism and cars and houses. You're sick if you care about those things. I'm not opposed to some of the multiculturalist and feminist agendas, but it's something that filmmakers who focus on sociological issues and institutions need to pon-der—that our imaginations, our dreams, our emotions are the only things that really matter. You can have all the equal-pay-for-equal-work statutes in the world, but if your imagination is impoverished, you are poorer than a ghetto kid squealing in the spray from a fire hydrant. *Treasure Island* and *The Arabian Nights* have more to say to a child's soul than a whole library of *I Have Two Mommies* and *My Uncle Lives with a Man* books. We need films that recognize that what a teenage girl thinks and feels and dreams is far more important than the clothes she wears or the car she drives. That's why *My Brilliant Career* is greater than *Clueless*.

Even most of the children's films I've seen have adopted our culture's depraved adult values. The kids in them are just little adults. Their minds and hearts do not represent an alternative to adult values, but a miniatur-ization of them—right down to the smutty adult leers the little boys give the little girls. They are just tiny capitalists, and the goal seems to be to turn the kids watching them into little consumers too—as they run off to McDonald's to collect mugs, action figures, and stickers. In other words, the emotions kid's films tap into are just as meaningless and self-destructive as the ones in adult movies.

Doing It

Friedman: What does the future hold for indie filmmakers with the rise of desktop filmmaking? Do you see any interesting filmmakers out there working in digital video?

Carney: All of the young filmmakers I know are working in digital, since they can't afford film! Well, maybe not all, but most of them. I think Andrew Bujalski is a hold-out. The obvious advantage of digital is that you can massively over-shoot. I just got off the phone with a friend who told me he had thirty hours of footage to work with to build his new movie out of. It would have been out of the question to buy and process that much 16mm film.

The downfall of most low-budget indie work is the acting. By necessity, young filmmakers usually have to use students, relatives, and other non-actors in their work. If they are limited to one or two takes because of the cost of film and processing, the results can be embarrassing. Massive over-shooting allows them to compensate. They can shoot until their actors are too tired to "act" or put down their actorly mannerisms, and start being real. My friend said he even shot some stuff like a documentarian, filming his actors when they weren't acting, when they didn't realize they were being filmed. Cassavetes did the same thing. It can make a real difference. As Renoir said, the whole scene is saved when the girl playing the servant thinks the shot is over and lets out a sigh.

When you don't have to worry about an eleven minute mag, you can do a scene over and over again. You can take chances. You can improvise. You can have fun, play around, experiment. Chaplin shot this way and it's always good for the work. Having a smaller crew and more portable equipment can also make things less intimidating. The mood is different—not so scary and formal and unnatural. The camera and crew aren't as obtrusive. And, of course, the PC has revolutionized editing, to take away a little of the time pressure and cost from that part of the process as well.

Technology Does Nothing

The new Sony and JVC HDV cameras are amazing. Near 35mm quality in a $5000 camera. Commercial high-definition TV-station quality. And Avid has a new editing program that you can work on it with in post. So anyone can really make a feature film now. A high-quality feature film at used car prices as Rick Schmidt puts it. But, but, but... no matter how cheap film-making becomes, there won't ever be a glut of masterpieces. Technology does nothing by itself. Did composers write better music or music criticism suddenly improve when cheap recording and playback methods became available? Did film criticism suddenly improve because of the invention of the VCR and DVD? Did architectural design programs result in better build-ings being built? If technology made people smarter and more sensitive, the second half of the twentieth century should have seen the greatest flower-ing of creativity in the history of art. Instead we know most music, paint-ing, architecture, and film got worse.

Better, smaller, cheaper cameras don't make better films; better filmmak-ers do. The digital revolution will probably quadruple the number of feature films shot and edited in a given year, but most of them will still be garbage, just like most of them are now. Look at the first video revolution ten or fif-teen years ago—when Beta SP and Hi-band 8 became cheap. What is its legacy? Porno flicks. There won't be any more artists born in a given year just because movies become cheaper to make. That particular form of insanity is in your DNA, and you either have it or you don't. Pen and paper are the ultimate low-budget technology, but how many great novels and plays and poems are written every year? I don't see a stream of Shakespeares being produced just because writing is inexpensive. Emotional clichés still lurk like land mines waiting to destroy you.

As a violinist friend used to say, it's a poor musician who blames his instru-ment. A real artist can use whatever is available. Picasso could have creat-ed masterpieces with a burnt stick and a piece of chalk. In fact he did. They're called charcoals. Cassavetes could have used a cheap, old-fash-ioned VHS camera and created scenes that were worth watching. In fact he did. In the last ten years of his life he filmed scenes that way at home just for the fun of doing it. Michael Almereyda made three amazing movies with a Pixel-cam, a sixty-nine dollar toy video camera for kids: *Another Girl, Another Planet, The Rocking Horse Winner,* and a documentary about the Sundance film festival.

It's a faulty analysis that locates the problem in the cost of the production. The harder nut to crack is distribution. How does a young, unknown filmmaker get a movie into a theater or onto mainstream TV—the internet doesn't count; the internet is a joke—no matter how it is made? The rub, of course, is that the more original the work, the harder it will be to sell it to the corporations that run those enterprises. It might not be "entertaining" enough. It might require you to think a little. It might be different. Or the worst sin of all in our culture of complaint: It might offend someone—another name for forcing them to think.

The life-or-death struggle every artist fights is not with technology but with our commercial culture. The businessmen, the accountants, the advertising guys always want to get their fingers in the pie—suggesting cuts, trying to speed up the pacing, pandering to some imaginary demographic—and if you let them convince you to make a single change, it's the death of personal expression. If anyone ever tells you to do something because someone else won't understand what you've done, you know they are talking nonsense. Generic truth—what "they" want, need, or feel—is not truth anymore. Truth can only be what you feel. The more personal your work, the more idiosyncratic and eccentric, the more truth there is in it. What's the Emerson quote? "Speak your most private, secret, personal thought, and you speak to all." When you try to speak for everyone, you speak for no one.

The distribution problem won't go away and I don't have a solution for it. If I did, I could go on TV and sell "how to get rich quick" kits. [Laughs] All I can tell you is that every week I get videos in the mail that are better than anything on HBO or PBS, accompanied with painful, personal letters describing how the filmmakers can't get them screened or distributed. The indie films that get lucky, the ones you hear about, are almost always picked up for the wrong reasons—not because of their intrinsic merit, but because they deal with some flash-in-the-pan topical theme, have sexual content, or appeal to a special-interest demographic—blacks or feminists or whomever. If you don't play to a special interest, forget it. When an edgy indie film about the Ku Klux Klan or middle school sex or high school violence gets picked up, it's not a vote for art; it's a business calculation of how many talk shows the distributor thinks the director can get onto because of the hot button issue. That's why most of the people who claim to want to help the indie movement are actually part of the problem.

Friedman: What do you mean?

Carney: I'll give you an example of how screwed up the support system for indie film is. I already mentioned Andrew Bujalski as an artist whose work I admire. Well let me tell you the story of how I first came across his work and what happened after that. I got a tape of his first film, Funny Ha Ha, in the mail a few years ago, along with a note saying that he couldn't get it screened anywhere. Nobody was interested. It's not that uncommon a story. Nobody was interested. It's not that uncommon a story. I hear it all the time. Almost exactly the same thing happened with Caveh Zahedi's *Little Stiff,* which I got it in the mail with the same kind of note attached to it: "Please look at my movie. I can't get it screened anywhere. Nobody is interested in it. Can you help me?"

Well, I looked at *Funny Ha Ha* and thought it was wonderful. It's a study of emotional clumsiness and imaginative confusion among the young and aimless, but better than Harmony Korine, because it was not about Diane Arbus gargoyles but recognizable people. The characters were just as twitchy and odd as Harmony's, but less exaggerated, in other words: closer to life, truer than Harmony's. And to make it even more interesting, the main character is a young woman and Bujalski really understood and appreciated her point of view. That's almost unprecedented for a male filmmaker—and totally beyond Harmony's capability.

Anyway, just as I had done after I viewed Caveh's tape, I went into action to try to help Andrew out. I sent him a quote to use on his web site; I made a few phone calls; I sent a few letters and emails to theater and festival programmers. Now this is where the story gets interesting. Remember nobody but nobody wanted the film to start with, but a few weeks later the buzz has gotten going and everything has changed. Now everybody wants the movie. The funny thing is that many of these people are the exact same ones who turned down, or refused to look at, Bujalski's film six months earlier, before I wrote or called them and told them how great it was. And now they love it. Isn't that funny? Critics and programmers are such sheep. They just need to be told what to like. You just have to tell them, and then everything is OK. Isn't that sick? Anyway, back to the main story: Now that everyone has changed their minds about his, Bujalski calls me and tells me he suddenly has three offers to screen it in Boston and one in another city. But guess what? Each programmer wants him to turn down the others. Each one says he doesn't want the movie unless he can be the first to screen it. The argument is the usual one about the smallness of the audience for indie film and how hard it is to sell tickets and how this particular programmer needs exclusivity to cash in on any reviews that appear.

Do you see how sick that is? The programmers claim to want to help the indie, but the only person they really want to help is themselves. They act like the filmmaker owes them something for showing the movie he poured his blood into and they didn't put up a penny for. This goes on all the time— at Sundance, the New York Film Festival, Cannes. They all want you to give them your movie first so they can get the glory and the reviews. And most indies end up agreeing to their terms. The theaters and festivals have the filmmakers, who are absolutely desperate for a screening, over a barrel and take advantage of it.

Friedman: So what is a filmmaker to do?

Carney: Every indie has to resist this kind of squeeze play for the good of all of the others in the future. I told Bujalski to tell the bookers that none of them could have his movie unless they agreed to his terms, which would include playing it everywhere he wants to, whenever he wants to. If all of the independent filmmakers did that in a given year, the indie theater and festival bookers would have to cave in. What are they going to do? Not show any films that year? I'm sure he didn't dare take my advice.

Bujalski's situation also illustrates the futility of paying an entrance fee and sending a video as a cold submission to a film festival. It's like sending an unsolicited manuscript to a publisher. Almost no one gets published or screened that way. It's practically all done by word-of-mouth recommendation. Only chumps play by the rules and pay the fees. But of course the festivals will be the last ones to tell you this. Right up to Cannes and Sundance, they maintain the pious fiction that anybody can get in. It just ain't so. You have to be known to them or your film has to come with a powerful recommendation. Ask me sometime about the student Academy Awards screenings I've been on the jury for. I don't know whether to laugh or cry about how they are run.

The Path of Rhetoric

Friedman: You explain in your Cassavetes on Cassavetes book that Cassavetes had this "mind's eye view" of himself, which is defined as how you perceive yourself before "society forces compromises or self-censorship on you." What filmmakers today seem to hold true to their mind's eye view?

Carney: I've given up on most of the established directors. Like most of my students, they're "camera happy"—in love with fancy visuals, editing tricks, and other forms of stylistic razzle-dazzle. Most directors are rhetoricians. They were trained to be that way in film school and almost all of their viewing experience has reinforced the training. They have been seduced away from truth in the pursuit of gaudy effects.

My hope is in the actors. Actors, by the nature of their calling, have a simpler, purer conception of expression. They have dedicated their lives to small, personal expressions. That's why many of them are willing to work for nothing in an independent film, just for a chance to be able to do something interesting and creative for a change. And some of them have become filmmakers by default, out of disgust with the roles offered to them in mainstream movies. Many of the most interesting recent American directors are, in fact, actors. I'm thinking of people like Tom Noonan, Steve Buscemi, Sean Penn, Vince Gallo, Tim Roth, and Gary Oldman. Their work is interested in truth, not style.

The other group of directors who have a commitment to truth-telling is documentarians. They have the same allegiance to truth over rhetoric. It's in their training as documentarians.

Friedman: Are you saying that documentary films are better than fictional ones?

Carney: That happens to be generally true in our culture, but that wasn't the point I was making. I meant that when documentary filmmakers make the transition to fiction film, they generally make better movies than born-in-the-bone dramatic directors. Someone who comes from a documentary background is less prone to hype-up the story with a lot of fancy stylistics.

Welles and Hitchcock and the critics and reviewers who championed their work took American film down the wrong road—the path of rhetoric. American critics and viewers have absurdly overvalued gaudy visual and acoustic effects ever since—from De Palma and Lynch to Stone, the Coen brothers, and Tarantino. Documentary filmmakers are finally doing an about-face, taking film back in the right direction, toward truth. But not all of them! [Laughs] There's always Errol Morris—whose documentaries are as seductive and deceitful as a Spielberg film.

Making a Life

Friedman: In this time of economic hardship, what do you recommend for people just entering a career in filmmaking?

Carney: I'm always uncomfortable with the notion of a "career" in anything. American society is structured so that it opulently rewards certain roles (lawyers, doctors, celebrity actors and athletes, wheeler-dealer businessmen, con-man stockbrokers, big-talking producers) and ignores or financially penalizes others (teachers, nurses, mothers, caregivers, ministers, artists). That never changes, in good times or bad.

We focus too much on the financial side. That's Hollywood thinking. If you are a real artist, you can make art with no money. Red Grooms used house paint and plywood to make his art. Paul Zaloom sets up a card table and moves toy soldiers around. Todd Haynes used Barbie dolls. I know a guy, Freddie Curchack, who made finger-shadows on a sheet as his art. An artist who complains about not having enough money is not an artist, but a businessman.

The only reason to make a movie, paint a painting, or write a poem is to try to understand something that matters to you that you don't understand. God knows, it's only the reason I write my books. If I were in it for the money, the fame, or the glory, I would have thrown in the towel and declared bankruptcy a long time ago! [Laughs] You do for the challenge and fun of picking your way through a jungle of unresolved ideas and feelings. The filmmakers I know who don't have the twenty thousand dollars it takes to make a movie are busy writing short stories or putting on plays with their friends. The beauty of that is that when they are able to get things together to make a movie, they already have a head start on something to film. They have tested it by tinkering with it and writing it out. They have workshopped it and seen where it needs to be revised. I tell students who say they can't afford a digital camera and sound equipment to put on a play in their living rooms or hide out in their basements and write a novel. If they tell me they're not interested in doing that, then I know they're not artists. They are more interested in having a career than a life.

Friedman: But they have to make a living.

Carney: I know that, but all I can deal with is the education side of it, and education is not about making a living, but making a life. A deep, spiritually meaningful life. It is a time for exploration and discovery. You're right. Every day after my students graduate, the world will be demanding its pound of flesh from them. There will be pressures placed on them to compromise, to put their values aside and do things the established way, the way that makes money, the way that makes for worldly success. That's why a university is such a special place. It is their one opportunity to do something for truth. Not for money. Not to get ahead. Not to curry favor with someone. Not to please anyone but themselves. It is a special time of life, a unique opportunity to go as far as they can, to dig as deep as they dare into the meaning of life. It is a time to study their hearts and souls and not worry about the ridiculous, wasteful, stupid things the world wants them to care about. To go to school to try build a resume, or to learn secrets about how to get rich or famous is to waste this glorious opportunity to break free from that oppressive system. The only right reason to go to school or to make art or to study art is to begin to understand truths the world suppresses and denies, and eventually to be able to share your understandings with others in acts of love and giving.

Just this afternoon I just spoke at a Boston U. open house "visiting day" for grad students who were visiting a number of different schools, and told them if some teacher or Dean stood up in a meeting and told them that if they got a degree from their school they could be rich or famous some day, they should run for the door. I told them that the only reason to go to grad school was to have a chance to explore themselves and our crazy, messed up culture so that they might begin to understand themselves and it—and eventually be able to communicate that understanding to others. To do anything else is to waste your education, and ultimately to waste your life. It is to sell your soul to the devil. Life is not about making money or getting famous or being successful. In our brief time here we must try to understand who we are and what really matters, and try to bring our feelings of love and kindness and understanding to others to change the world for the better in some way. That's what school is about—or what it should be about. Starting out on—or continuing—that great adventure of discovery and self-discovery.

Film School

Friedman: Sometimes it seems like we have a very "everyone for themselves" attitude in the film industry in the U.S., which leaves little room

for cultivating a master-student relationship. Also, to be unique and pro-
gressive as an artist often seems to imply to trash, not build upon, the
past. Do you agree with this observation, and if you do, do you see any
filmmakers out there trying to build upon a sense of film tradition and his-
tory in their individual styles?

Carney: Rob Nilsson said something very interesting in a Res column. He
said that film schools should be abolished and all the young people should
go find some low-budget independent filmmaker whose works they loved,
apprentice themselves to him or her, and give their tuition money to the
filmmaker. Of course, the proposal was tongue in cheek. He knows it will
never happen, and that it sounds insane to most people. But I would love to
have young filmmakers take him seriously. It could change the history of
American film. I've given my students this advice, but they always think I'm
joking.

Film school is a waste of time for most students. In fact, it's counter-pro-
ductive in most cases because the wrong things are taught—like explaining
away your characters' mysteries by providing unnecessary background information, and how to keep the stupid plot moving along. Why should every
movie look like every other movie? Even children's books are more different
from one another than Hollywood films are. Who says you have to have
establishing shots or over-the-shoulder shots? Who says a scene has to be
lighted or edited in a certain way? It really shows contempt for the art.
You'd never tell a musician he had to compose for particular instruments
and play in certain keys, or a painter what colors to use or what size canvas
to paint on. And what happens at the end of the process? Another class of
know-nothings is turned loose in the world to compete with each other for a
Hollywood distribution deal.

To tell the truth, most of the students I teach give up on film after they
leave school. They go into something else. It's the open secret of most film
programs. The faculty tell the parents all these tall-tales about careers in
film on visiting day before their children enroll, but most of the film students stop doing film the day they graduate. And the ones who go to LA and
fight to get a job and starve for a while end up pushing a dolly or stringing
wires on some big budget production that no one involved with gives a
damn about. Those are the lucky ones! For that you went to four years of
film school? To learn how to push a dolly or answer the phone for some producer?

Each of these students could have made their own feature their own way if they had taken Nilsson's advice and apprenticed themselves to an indie filmmaker. Instead they go off to work in a factory every morning, and become a tiny cog in an enormous studio machine.

What a waste of an education. What a waste of a life. They had it right in the sixteenth century. The guild system was a much better way to learn art.

The University

Friedman: Why do you think so many filmmakers are drawn to teaching, besides the schedule flexibilities?

Carney: [Laughs] Well, they have to pay the rent somehow, and the hourly rate is a few cents better than McDonald's! Lots of filmmakers become teachers so they can use equipment for free or get students to help them with their films. But I'd like to think there is a higher, nobler reason—the dream of being part of a community of like-minded, soulful, spiritual searchers. Universities are the last of the monasteries—the last shelter from the capitalist way of measuring everything in terms of popularity and profit. That makes them a wonderful place to be.

Of course I'm talking about an ideal university. There are so few of them left. Most academic film programs—all of the best-known ones, NYU, UCLA, USC, and the others—do not represent an alternative to the business sickness of our culture, but are devoted to training people to enter and compete within it. The students don't ask questions about the meaning of art and life. They major in vocational ed—no different from studying auto mechanics or farming or being in beautician school. Like I was saying, they'd rather give their students a job than a life.

I get emails every week from students who have spent four years majoring in film at UCLA or USC or NYU, and have never heard the name of a single one of the art filmmakers I write or speak about mentioned in their classes. The so-called independent films shown in their courses are by mainstream directors like Steven Spielberg, Oliver Stone, and John Sayles. Artistic expression is represented by someone like Hitchcock. The students should be awarded degrees in advertising and promotion when they graduate. That's the only area the work of these filmmakers represents. They're not studying art but commerce.

The reason I'm so familiar with these problems is that they are not taking place in a galaxy far away from me. The Boston University film program is no different from the UCLA one in this respect, maybe it's worse. Just because I am in it doesn't mean that the program reflects my personal values. I have to remind saucer-eyed students about this when they write me and say they want to come to Boston University "to study with me." Like I was Yoda! I tell them that they will also have to study with a lot of people who disagree with me, who argue with me, who think I'm a pain in the neck. Boston U. churns out worker bee drones for the studio hive the same as other programs do.

As far as my own personal effort to present alternatives to Hollywood values in my course offerings goes, it's pretty puny. And I'm losing the battle. For about a year now, I've been getting constant criticism from a newly appointed administrator at Boston University—I don't want to embarrass him by giving his name or title—about the elitism and smallness of the film studies graduate program, as well as the fact that the curriculum downplays—or outright ignores—Hollywood movies. This guy has applied terrific pressure to make the admission process less selective, the course content more pop-culturish, and the grading standards easier. He's told me he wants me to admit three or four times the number of students I have in the past and not to have such high standards in terms of their writing and thinking ability. And he's told me over and over again that he thinks the courses should take a less critical stance toward Hollywood.

I've sat down with him and tried to explain the value of the program as it presently exists. I've told him how few jobs there are, how tight the Ph.D. field is, and how irresponsible it is to be turning out large numbers of degree-recipients who won't be able to do anything with their degree. But he just doesn't get it. His academic background is in a completely different field, and he knows nothing about film or film criticism. He has no idea how bad most film criticism is, and no clue why a small, high-quality artistic program might be preferable to a big, schlocky, pop-culture one. In terms of Hollywood film, as far as I can tell, he thinks I'm out of my mind not to be teaching movies that are playing at the malls and metroplexes and not to be admitting students who want to devote their lives to watching them or writing about them.

A few months ago, after a year of tussling, as I balked at his suggestions to make voluntary changes, he took matters into his own hands and laid down graduate admissions guidelines that effectively take the admissions process out of my control and force the program to admit large numbers of academically less qualified and more Hollywood-oriented students.

Friedman: Can he make you change what you teach or who you admit into the program? What about academic freedom?

Carney: A university is no different from the larger culture. There's a first amendment out there too. That means in theory you can say or do almost anything. But theory is different from practice. Capitalism prevents you from doing a lot of what the first amendment allows. In academia, no one will hire you or publish your writing if your ideas are too original or different. And if you self-publish your work—I've done that—and can't afford to advertise and distribute the result, no one will buy it because no one will know it exists. The power of the purse makes sure we don't get too frisky with our freedoms.

To answer your question: after he saw I wouldn't budge, this guy called a meeting of the film studies faculty and said that he intended to cut back funding if we didn't do things his way. Then he told us we should meet and take a vote on what we wanted to do. Do you see how clever that is? "I'm going to take away your money if you don't go along with me. Now go off and tell me what you've decided to do." Might as well live in North Korea. That's how Kim Jon Il governs! [Laughs]

Don't forget, I'm not Napoleon or a third-world dictator. No matter what I think, I have to consult with my faculty. So we had our meeting. I urged taking a stand to defend our high admissions standards, our small class sizes, our focus on art film, and our stringent grading, but I got outvoted. In fact, I was the only one on that side of any of the issues. Everyone else voted to go along with the administrator. No surprise there. He had told us what he preferred and that our budget was at stake if we went against his wishes. Some of the others are angling for promotions. All of them are aware that future pay raises will be determined by this guy. It was an easy decision for them.

When personal considerations are at risk, abstract intellectual issues suddenly become a little less clearly defined in peoples' minds. As Bush's election shows, people vote their self-interest, even as they tell you—and are absolutely convinced that—they are voting their morals.

It was a good experience for me to have. A good lesson to learn. Everyone had wonderful reasons for why they decided to go along with this guy. Great justifications. And they were completely sincere. They all really, truly, deeply believed that they were making the right decision. That includes this administrator. He is convinced that he is improving the program by "broadening" it. He is proud of what he is doing. Every time I see him, he reminds me how unrealistic and elitist my vision of the film program was, and teases me about how Boston University is "not Oxford or Cambridge."

The whole process has been fascinating to live through, a real life-lesson. It's amazing to see how people can fool themselves. What makes filmmakers like Cassavetes and Noonan and Kramer so deep is that they find ways to dramatize these states of well-intentioned self-delusion. It's never the way Hollywood presents it. No one has bad intentions. No one ever thinks they are doing wrong. People who make awful decisions never realize they are awful. They are convinced down to the soles of their shoes that they are doing the correct thing. That applies to this administrator. Heck, it even applies to Bin Laden. I'm not equating the two! [Laughs]

The University as Supermarket

Friedman: What about the students? Won't they object?

Carney: Unfortunately not. The ones admitted who would have been rejected in previous years, which is two thirds of them, are delighted to get in. And, in terms of the course content, all but a very small number of students will probably be happier with more Hollywood movies in the curriculum. It's not hard to understand. What do they know? They come into school having been brainwashed by the media into believing figures like Spielberg and Tarantino are as good as film gets. They've never heard of Tarkovsky or Ozu or Bresson or Kiarostami or Rappaport. They don't know the great works of art. They'll never realize what they are missing.

Of course everything that I am saying goes against the grain of post-60s cultural assumptions that students should have the final say about what they study. We live in a democracy where things are supposed to be decided by popularity. That's how we elect our leaders. What's popular is what's stocked in stores and what gets reported in our newspapers. But that's not how a university should work. It's a mistake to teach films that the students want you to teach. It's a mistake to put works on the syllabus because they are popular or will get a large enrollment. If you teach what the students have heard of and want to see, you might as well open a movie theater in the mall. My job is to show the students movies that they haven't heard of, movies they don't know they want to see, movies that do things in ways they've never even imagined a work can do them. The music department knows this. The art department knows this. The English department knows this. The physics and math departments know this. They don't consult students' wishes when they create a syllabus. They aren't afraid to force students to do things they'd never do on their own. But the film department is always, at least implicitly, playing to the audience—organizing courses around films that have gotten the most attention over the years, and giving the students a kind of vote on what should be taught by evaluating courses in terms of their popularity and enrollment.

At the point they show up on campus, very few students have any conception of what art does. Half of them come into my classes treating film as a form of sociology or cultural history. They look at a movie to study the depiction of women or minority groups or gays or whatever, and they evaluate it based on how politically correct or incorrect it is. They take out their clipboards and work down the race/class/gender/ideology checklist.

The other half profess to care about artistic expression, but their understanding is based on these bogus pop culture notions of art. Many think art involves glamorous photography, lush sound effects, and beautiful settings. Some think it is about creating powerful emotions. If it makes you feel something, it must be great art. Others think works of art are always "unrealistic" in some way—that art involves creating visionary- or dream-states by using fancy lighting effects, weird music, or jumpy editing. Others think art is about employing metaphors and various kinds of color or shape symbolism. Others think art is about telling stories in convoluted, non-chronological ways. Others think it's about sneaking in hidden meanings and surprise endings. I understand where both groups are coming from. It's what they've been taught. They've learned this stuff from teachers and from viewing a lot of bad movies. Movies by Hitchcock, Welles, Spielberg, Lucas, Lynch, De Palma, Tarantino, and the Coen brothers.

And I don't want to seem to be picking on students. A lot of people have the same limited views of art. Artistic appreciation is a very rare thing in our culture because exposure to art is a very rare thing in our culture. Look at the books people read, the music they listen to, the movies they enjoy! I travel a lot and almost always ask the person sitting next to me what they are reading or what kind of music they like. Maybe one in a hundred people has any interest in or familiarity with art. Maybe it's fewer than that. It doesn't matter how many years they have attended school, what they majored in, or what degrees they hold.

Fear of Flying

My painful, awkward, fun job—it really is a lot of fun!—is to force my students to let go of their limited understandings of art. Classes are great, exciting, crazy tugs-of-war. They try to stay on their feet and I try to pull the rug out from under them. To show them works that don't yield to these ways of understanding, works of real art that do much more complex, slippery, challenging things. But it's an uphill battle. The force of the whole culture is arrayed against it. The students generally don't appreciate the works I show or begin to understand how they function until we have put in a lot of time together. It can take months. One of my courses runs 70 hours over fourteen weeks, and that's frequently not enough time to do what I want to do. I get emails every week from students who have been out of school for a few years who tell me that only then are they finally beginning to see what I was trying to show them.

Friedman: What about the grad students? They must be more sophisticated.

Carney: Oh, the grad students are worse than the undergrads in this respect. They have a lot of time and effort—a lot of ego—invested in their admiration of *Mulholland Drive* and *Vertigo* and *Blue Velvet* and *Pulp Fiction,* and fight me tooth and nail when I try to show them the limitations of those sorts of works. What I am doing threatens their whole world view. It makes me understand the Marine Corps commitment to getting them when they are 18. [Laughs] An 18-year-old is a lot easier to teach—to inspire or scare into thinking in new ways. People in their mid-twenties or thirties don't want to have to think new ideas. They dig in their heels when you try to move them in a new direction.

Do you know the quote by Guillaume Appolinaire? "'Come to the edge,' he said. 'We are afraid,' they said. 'Come to the edge,' he said; and slowly, reluctantly, they came. He pushed them. And they flew." It's hard to overcome the fear of falling. I mean the fear of flying.

You also have to take into account who goes into grad school to study film. There are some exceptions, thank God, but in general a student who decides to get a graduate degree in film is someone who took a lot of film courses as an undergrad and did well at them. They are people who chose to take courses dealing with *The Godfather, Blade Runner,* and *Psycho* rather than the paintings of Rembrandt, the music of Bach, the poetry of Emily Dickinson, or the prose of Henry James. What does that tell you? It tells me a lot, and it's borne out by my experience when they come into my courses. Most of them are not readers, not deep thinkers, not interested in serious art, and generally not independent intellects in any sense—or they wouldn't have done so well in those undergraduate film courses writing papers about *2001* and *Citizen Kane.* They spent their college careers watching junky movies and writing junky papers in praise of them. It sounds like a horrible thing for a film professor to say, but having been a film major is generally not a very high recommendation for the state of their emotional development and intellectual potential. You can't be a very sophisticated person and take *Kill Bill, Schindler's List,* or *Boogie Nights* seriously or want to devote your life to viewing works like these. That's why I often try to admit people who have majored in things other than film as undergraduates.

I should say, tried. Those days are past. I recently tendered my resignation as director of the program. I'll step down this summer. It's funny. It was another illustration of how Hollywood gets it all wrong. Resigning wasn't some kind of big moral victory. The guy I've been jousting with didn't take my resignation as a courageous stand or a principled response to the changes he had made. He took it as my concession that he had won the battle and I was surrendering. He was absolutely delighted to have me step down.

Friedman: A fun question: If you could make one film required curriculum for American film students, what would it be and why? Why is this film innovative or unique?

Carney: If I were limited to teaching one two- or three-hour film class for all eternity, one shot to change the history of American film, I wouldn't show any movies! I'd have the students listen to Bach's D-minor Double Violin Concerto or his Goldberg Variations and ask them to try to get that into their work. Or discuss some Eudora Welty or Alice Munro short stories. Or read some Stanley Elkin. Or some of D.H. Lawrence's criticism. He is the greatest critic of any art in the last hundred years, but I defy you to find a single film theory class that reads him. They'd rather read Jonathan Culler or David Bordwell! Or I'd have them look at Degas. Those are things I already do in my classes and I'm convinced that many of the students learn more from doing them than they do from looking at any movie.

If you absolutely required me to screen something, I'd use my three hours to show short films. They are better than most features, and would at least demonstrate that a movie doesn't necessarily have to tell a stupid "story," be "entertaining," or any of that other rot Hollywood would make us believe.

Friedman: *What would you show?*

Carney: Fran Rizzo's *Sullivan's Last Call*, Bruce Conner's *Permian Strata, Valse Triste, Take the 5:10 to Dreamland,* and *A Movie;* Jay Rosenblatt's *Human Remains, Pregnant Moment, I Used to be a Filmmaker,* and *Restricted;* Su Friedrich's *Sink or Swim* and *Rules of the Road;* Shirley Clarke's *Portrait of Jason;* Mike Leigh's *Afternoon, Sense of History,* and *The Short and Curlies;* Charlie Weiner's *Rumba.* And ten minutes from Tom Noonan's *What Happened Was,* Caveh Zahedi's *A Little Stiff,* Mark Rappaport's *Local Color* or *Scenic Route,* and Elaine May's *Mikey and Nicky.* That's should be about three or four hours of stuff. If there was a little more time, I'd add selected chunks from Bresson's *Lancelot of the Lake* or *Femme Douce,* Renoir's *Rules of the Game,* Tarkovsky's *Sacrifice* or *Stalker,* Barbara Loden's *Wanda,* John Korty's *Crazy Quilt,* Ozu's *Late Spring,* or the last ten minutes of his *Flavor of Green Tea over Rice.*

The least the students would learn is that a film doesn't have to look like a Hollywood movie. That, no matter how much *Entertainment Tonight* and *The New York Times* try to persuade us otherwise, Hollywood is a tiny and ultimately unimportant rivulet flowing away from the great sea of art. The smart ones would learn something about artistic structure and how the greatest movies use something other than action to keep us caring and in the moment—that the worst way to make a movie is to organize it around a gripping, suspenseful plot. Plot, actions, and narrative events are the biggest lies we can tell about what life is really about. As Tom Noonan said to my students, just the way you say hello to a friend or shake someone's hand is enough to build a scene around. Life is a string of those kinds of moments. Why are we always looking for something else to happen? Why do we feel our lives are not already interesting enough to make art out of?

Ray Carney would like to thank Marty Jobe for assisting with the editing of the interview transcript.

THE TORRENT

Drenching in the media flow

by Todd Gitlin

The media saturates, drenches, overflows our lives: an endless torrent of words, images, sounds. This is not the "information age", a mere channel to life, says Gitlin, but life itself. How do people make sense of the onrush without being submerged by it?

Readers of openDemocracy (www.opendemocracy.net) will, I hope, have consulted the lucid debate in the Media strand on the impact of giant conglomerates and whether they are a threat to democracy. My own thinking about media has evolved toward a different (not necessarily incompatible) set of questions about the experience of media and their saturation of everyday life. They have created a civilization obsessed with speed. What are the strategies which everyone uses to try and cope with saturation and speed? And what are the dynamics behind the spread of this way of life beyond the borders of the United States—indeed, beyond any borders at all?

The swarming enormity of popular culture is obvious. Never have so many communicated so much, on so many screens, through so many channels, absorbing so many hours of irreplaceable human attention. And most of this is itself about communications. Whenever strangers wish to feel out common ground and establish that they are not altogether alien to each other, they compare notes on stars and shows. They deploy the latest catch phrases, and in America indicate that they are *West Wing*, *South Park*, *Oprah*, Howard Stern, *World Wrestling Federation,* or Rush Limbaugh types of people. In other societies other soap operas, shows and stars fulfill the same function.

In all their bits and chunks, the media are major subjects of the media themselves, glutted as they are with reviews, profiles, commentaries, gossip, trivia and bulletins about hits and celebrities, rising and falling stars, blazing and cooling fads, trends and gadgets, the ebb and flow of executive careers in the media, the latest in media corporate acquisitions of other media corporations.

Entertainment writers and talking heads are legion. *The New York Times'* weekly section, "Circuits," devoted to new communications technology, has been emulated elsewhere. Claims of "media effects" circulate through television, newspaper columns, and the internet. Organizations galore sponsor conferences galore on violence and profanity in the media. Books and journals about the media stream off the presses.

Yet for all the talk, and all the talk about the talk, the main truth about the media slips through our fingers. Critics and commentators miss the immensity of the experience of media, the sheer quantity of attention paid, the devotions and rituals that absorb our time and resources. Riding the torrent, they don't see it as a torrent and instead talk and argue about the splashes and the spray. The obvious but hard-to-grasp truth is that living with the media is today one of the main things human beings do.

The centrality of media is disguised, in part, by the prevalence of that assured, hard-edged phrase "information society," or even, more grandly, "information age." Such terms are instant propaganda for a way of life which is also a way of progress.

Who in his right mind could be against information or want to be without it? Who wouldn't want to produce, consume, and accumulate more of this useful stuff, remove obstacles to its spread, invest in it, see better variants of it spring to life? Even today's Luddites want to obtain speedier internet access, put up more websites, promote more extensive listservs, publish more tracts, and otherwise diffuse more information about the dangers of high technology. "Information society" glows with a positive aura. The very term "information" points to a gift—specific and ever-replenished, shining forth in the bright light of utility. Ignorance is not bliss, information is.

I feel, therefore I am

But we diminish the significance of media and our reliance on them in everyday life by classifying them as channels of information. Media today are occasions for and conduits of a way of life identified with rationality, technological achievement, and the quest for wealth, but also for something else entirely, something we call "fun," "comfort," "convenience," or "pleasure."

We have come to care tremendously about how we feel and how readily we can change our feelings. Media are means to do this. We aim, through media, to indulge and serve our hungers by inviting images and sounds into our lives, making them come and go with ease in a never-ending quest for more and better entertainment.

Our prevailing business is the business not of information but of enjoyment, the feeling of feelings, to which we give as much time as we can manage, not only at home but in the car, at work, or walking down the street. We seek and sometimes find a laugh from a sitcom joke, an erotic twinge from an underwear ad, a jolt of rhythm from a radio playlist, a sensation of moving with remarkable speed through a video game. Even the quest for information includes the quest for the delight to be found in retrieving it—a quest, that is, for a feeling.

In a society that fancies itself the freest ever, spending time with communications machinery is the main use to which we have put our freedom. All human beings play, but this civilization has evolved a particular form of play: wedding fun to convenience by bathing ourselves in images and sounds.

The most important thing about the communications we live among is not that they deceive (which they do); or that they broadcast a limiting ideology (which they do); or emphasize sex and violence (which they do); or convey diminished images of the good, the true and the normal (which they do); or corrode the quality of art (which they also do); or reduce language (which they surely do)—but that with all their lies, skews, and shallow pleasures, they saturate our way of life with a promise of feeling.

Even if we may not know exactly how we feel—about one or another batch of images, we feel that they are there, streaming out of large screens and small, or bubbling in the background of life, but always coursing onward. To an unprecedented degree, the torrent of images, songs, and stories streaming has become our familiar, our felt world.

E pluribus, unum

Obliquely and unintentionally, we allude to the biggest truth about media with a grammatical error. We commonly speak of "the media" in the singular. Grammatical sticklers (like this writer) cringe when the media themselves, or college students reared on them (or it) speak of "the media" as they might speak of "the sky"—as if there were only one.

There is, however, a reason for this error other than grammatical slovenliness. Something in our experience makes us want to address media as "it." We may be confused about whether "the media" are or "is" technologies, or cultural codes—whether "television" is an electronic system for bringing images into the home, or the sum of its stars and channels; whether "the media" includes alternative rock or the Internet.

But through all the confusion we sense something like a unity at work. The torrent is seamless: a collage of back-to-back stories, talk-show banter, fragments of ads, soundtracks of musical snippets. Even as we click around, something feels uniform—a relentless pace, a pattern of interruption, a seriousness about unseriousness, a readiness for sensation, an anticipation of the next new thing. Whatever the diversity of texts, the media largely share a texture, even if it is maddeningly difficult to describe—real and unreal, present and absent, disposable and essential, distracting and absorbing, sensational and tedious, emotional and numbing.

In *Media Unlimited* I wrestle with the maddening difficulty. Take one aspect only: the 24/7 wraparound spectacles we know as O.J. Simpson, Princess Diana, John F. Kennedy Jr., Clinton-Lewinsky. They have a peculiar aspect that might help explain their appeal, their hold and their consequences.

During these episodes, people can feel not only enthralled, but relieved. The wraparound saga has the virtue of sluggishness which allows them to relax. The everyday onrush of lightweight fluff grinds into slow motion as the anchor declares breathlessly, "This just in". Commentators expostulate, epiphanies arrive—moments of revelation and showdown, partial resolutions, true and false leads—but in the main, padded by "backstory," the story moves glacially. Like a soap opera, it does not require rapt attention. The "real" news, the "latest," will recycle at the top of the hour, if not sooner.

Meanwhile, for example, during the search for the young Kennedy's plane, the screen read "Breaking News". But it showed boats crisscrossing a placid Nantucket Sound, looking for debris as the camera showed only open water. During the state funeral, the wedding, the hijacking, longueurs take over. The impounded plane sits on the runway. The reporter at O.J. Simpson's mansion reports breathlessly that nothing is going on. Amid the stasis, a few iconic images recycle endlessly; the Challenger explodes, O.J.'s white Bronco cruises down the freeway, the Murrah Building in Oklahoma City stands as an instant ruin, the fireman holds the dead child, Monica Lewinsky hugs President Clinton at the rope line, Clinton points his finger and denies having sex "with that woman," and now hijacked jets smash again and again into the Twin Towers.

The pundits, barking heads, hunt for amusing or pontifical sidebars, striving to summon the nation to feelings all of us are supposed to feel, trying to power the display with emotional bursts that the pictures usually themselves do not engender.

In a genuine ongoing emergency—like the aftermath of the World Trade Center and Pentagon attacks of 11 September, 2001—saturation coverage can carry much practical information. But mainly, emotions flow: grief, horror, anger, fear. No wonder steady viewers grow numb. Yet this feeling of stasis may be not so much a dramatic flaw as an attraction. The spectator's burden of choice is, for once, lifted. You are riveted, your choices made for you. You duck in and out, check "what's new." Your opinion is polled, your talk radio calls and e-mails are solicited. You may feel privileged to be "a witness to history."

Instant communities form on the Internet, jokes fly around the world via e-mail. The people you run into share an automatic agenda—even if high on that agenda is disgust with the excess of coverage, expression of that disgust being itself a predictable feature of saturation coverage.

The ritual of common preoccupation seems to justify the intensity of the coverage in a self-justifying, ongoing torrent that takes us along with it.

.

Y TU EXISTENTIALISM TAMBIEN?

An existential renaissance anybody?

by Timothy Dugdale

"And your mother too"—so comes the final salvo of macho brinksmanship between two Mexican teenagers tippling immodestly at a cantina on an Oaxacan beach. Each has confessed to shagging the other's girlfriend. Now, their friendship in ruins, the gloves are really off. Fueled by mescal and testosterone, they try to outdo one another with boasts of sexual mischief and toasts to those boasts. Looking on (and egging them on) is Luisa, the Spanish-born erstwhile wife of one of the boy's cousins, a vainglorious upper-middle class pantywaist addicted to cheating on her and then whining about it.

Y Tu Mamá También begins as one might expect—with sex. Two teenagers are having at it in a comfortable looking bedroom under a poster for the film, *Harold and Maude* (1971). In between thrusts, the boy demands to know if the girl, leaving for a summer on the Continent, promises not to get it on with a variety of clichés torn from a European youth hostel—the french fag, the gringo backpacker and of course, the smelly Mexican selling bracelets in the street. Seemingly used to this kind of talk, she provides cheeky additions to his litany as she moves on top. The ante has been raised. A half-hearted promise of fidelity is made. As the camera pulls away from the lovers, an unseen narrator divulges that while the girl's mother, a French divorcee, doesn't mind her daughter sleeping with her boyfriend, Tenoch, his friend Julio has less luck. His girlfriend has a pediatrician and a Lacanian analyst for parents. The camera moves to their living room, a joyless sterile place where the father nervously feigns reading the newspaper as the wife hovers behind the sofa where Julio sips a juice. The narrator tells us the parents are split on Julio—the mother sees their relationship as innocent, the father disapproves. Upstairs, Cici can't find her passport. With the mother's blessing, Julio is dispatched. By now Cici has found her passport and lost her trackpants as she demands Julio shut the door and give her a sweet going-away present. Their coupling is a self-parody. The mother appears at the door. Cici throws Julio off the bed but he comes up smiling, passport in hand.

We move to the airport where the boys and girls are saying farewell. Tenoch confesses to Julio that he "can't stand this goodbye bullshit. Why don't they just go"? Meanwhile, the girls express their own desire to get to Europe already, albeit with more finesse. Ana's father appears. The narrator confides that he is a journalist who has begun dabbling in politics with Mexico's main opposition party. The father likes Tenoch but calls him the "preppie" when his daughter isn't around. As we hear this, we see the father take a call on his cell phone.

The boys are now left to their own devices. They drive around in Tenoch's sedan, provided by his father under the condition that he take economics at university. We join them as Tenoch's luxurious house for a joint and a few laughs with their stoner guru/dealer/partner-in-crime, Saba. The narrator reveals that Tenoch's father is some sort of bigwig in the ruling party. Overcome with patriotic fervor at the birth of his son, Tenoch was named after an Aztec emperor. Tenoch's mother arrives home, beautifully coiffed and resplendent in a flowing pantsuit. She has the air of a new age devotee, a suspicion confirmed in an aside from the narrator. After chiding the boys for smoking, she invites Julio to a family wedding that will allegedly be attended by the president of the country. Tellingly, she cautions Julio that he must be very well-dressed for the occasion.

It is at the wedding we meet the film's other crucial character. The boys quickly get loaded on clandestine *cuba libres* and start counting contemptuously the ridiculous number of bodyguards all the guests have brought with them. While Tenoch's father launches into a purple, self-serving toast to the president, the boys set their sights on a beautiful woman enjoying a quiet wine. Their mission is delayed by Tenoch's cousin, Jano, who tries to caution Tenoch about the burden of becoming a writer. Quickly tiring of his pretentious bullshit, the boys conspire to send him packing. Julo knocks a glass of wine on the bore's suit. Jano is led away by a fawning aunt. The boys move in for the kill. They chat up Luisa, telling her about a glorious beach called Boca de Cielo—Heaven's Mouth—that they are planning to visit. Does she want to come along?

No she doesn't. At least not until she takes a call from her husband who is at some academic conference. He tearfully confesses his infidelity. Unable to endure his confession, she hangs up. The next day she rings Tenoch, asking if the trip is still a go. Taken by surprise, the boy bullshits her. Sure, we'll pick you up. Tenoch rings Julio. They secure use of a beat up station wagon from Julio's sister (who was intending to take humanitarian aid to the rebels of Chapas), make a quick trip to a mega-supermarket to stock up on provisions (including, of course, condoms) and fetch Luisa.

If I have been overly descriptive, it is to point out the highly schematic structure of the film's "identity" politics. The boys are happy idiots, obsessed with performing for themselves and girls. In existential terms, they are pups frolicking in a well-padded incommensurability. Parents are either zombified bourgeoisie, invisible or in the case of Ana's father, sell-outs. And the narrator, in all his Godardian (Cuarón has admitted his admiration for *Masculin/Feminin* [1966]) glory, directs the viewer to facile, left-leaning observations, intended to add resonance to the action.

Indeed, the narrator with his detached tone and omniscience seems at first blush to be the voice of good faith, revealing truths that the characters refuse to acknowledge or simply cannot know. He is a surrogate, to paraphrase Camus, of "the absurd that may strike a man in the face at any street corner". The characters are locked in their little dramas; the narrator locates them in the larger, unforgiving context of the absurd. Moreover, the narrator is the director's agent of discontent, the voice of a man at the edge of middle age looking back at the portal of adulthood with mixed emotions. "I wish I had known... but to what cause"?

Julio and Tenoch are on the cusp of adulthood in Mexico, a country on the cusp of adulthood. The boys are on a journey with their country. But as much as this film is a coming-of-age tale, it is also a road movie. The existential crisis of the characters and the larger existential crisis of national "development" in a globalized economy are best articulated on the road between Mexico City and the Oaxacan beach.

One morning early into the trip, Tenoch enters Luisa's room to borrow some shampoo. She's crying but perhaps thankful for his presence, she asks him to remove his towel. Is she seducing him or taunting him? He willingly rises to her challenge but in his haste to ravish her, he comes quickly. Meanwhile, Julio broods in the motel's pool. The narrator announces that the last time Julio felt like this was when he witnessed his godfather making out with his mother. To battle back against his pal's good fortune, Julio tells Tenoch that he had an encounter with Tenoch's girl. The game is on. That night, the boys stage an inquisition, with Tenoch demanding every sordid detail from his pal and Julio, as the narrator reveals, keeps talking until the truth disappears. Or rather the possibility of truth disappears. After Julio has his own disastrous encounter in the backseat of the station wagon with Luisa, who seems to be trying to recalibrate the boy's friendship, Tenoch confesses to an indiscretion with Julio's moll.

"Truth exists" wrote Kierkegaard "only as the individual himself produces it in action". The lies that Julio and Tenoch tell each other about shagging the other's girlfriend are devastating to their friendship. Sartre's maxim that "hell is other people" is even more piquant amongst friends; if your friend is ultimately unknowable, at least friendship offers a tacit agreement of non-aggression and empathy. Without fraternity, hedonism puts you in the spotlight of existential isolation and keeps you there. A number of times, Tenoch and Julio exchange epithets—preppie, white trash—that invoke both national and international class warfare. How can these guys be true buddies if history won't let them? But then again, fraternity may be the last refuge of psychic autonomy against the "divide and conquer" strategies of global capitalism as it plunders and commodifies national youth cultures. Fraternity is refusal. To Marx. To McDonald's.

The boys' very shaky postures of machismo prevent them from seeing that they've been had by their own fantasies. To say that Luisa is some sort of *femme fatale* is wrong. In Truffaut's *Jules and Jim* (1962), the struggle for the lady is the linchpin of the film. Here it is a Trojan Horse; Luisa will have neither of the boys. We know she has their number from the very beginning, the way she invites their outrageous come-ons and then parries with salacious questions that force them to reveal their sexual callowness. When they gleefully recite their "astral cowboy manifesto"—a sort of Ten Commandments for teenage Mexican guys who love drugs, soccer and chicks—she feigns surprise and interest. It's a ploy of good faith though. She's trying to keep her tour guides amused as she searches for her answers to the "groundlessness" that's been thrust upon her. The world she had constructed for herself has revealed its lack of foundation. Like Mersault in Camus' *The Stranger*, she is making an eleventh-hour fight for freedom. Her life has been spent in the service of others. Unlike Mersault, she has lived a moral life, a moral life achieved through good works. Now she must live for herself.

The parched Mexican countryside is much more than a metaphor for the existential distress of the characters. Antonioni was a master of using the emptiness of city spaces and architecture to articulate the isolation of the individual and the capitulation of the individual into the ennui that the open spaces invited. And who can forget the final shot of *The Passenger* (1975) when the desert hotel where Jack Nicholson's doppelganger meets his demise in the blazing midday sun is shown in quiet repose at twilight. Alfonso Cuarón uses the Mexican landscape with equal aplomb. Oaxaca is, in fact, the inconvenient Mexico that sits between the boys' pampered niche in the city and the bourgeois fantasy of the virgin beach. The countryside is all too real. At one point, the camera offers a point-of-view shot as the car drives through some dreary small town, the streets lined with cantinas and auto-junkyards. A woozy melancholic Brian Eno song plays on the soundtrack. Then the radio stammers and dies. Culture is being sapped of its comforting energies by the forces of nature. The music that the boys have used to keep their jocularity on track is suddenly gone. Moments later, we see Tenoch making the unhappy connection between his own life and the fleeting glimpse of a sign marking the town from which his nanny came to tend to his every whim. Suddenly, he is in the moment, in the landscape, in the history of the country. Then, the car breaks down.

Bye Bye Brazil (1981), a film by Carlos Diegues, used the same road movie premise to discuss the impact of television on rural communities in northern Brazil and the displacement and provisional re-integration of older communication technologies and practices under the cathode ray tube regime. As a ragtag vaudeville troupe crosses the Brazilian outback in search of an audience untouched by television, they realize the battle is lost. No place is safe from the glowing beast; the troupe breaks up and scatters. At one point in *También,* Luisa places a call from a payphone in a dusty roadside bar. The camera cuts to her well-kept apartment where her message fills the empty rooms. She is saying goodbye to her husband but she is also saying goodbye to the false promise of communication technology—that human connections are inevitable and stable regardless of distance. They are not and the further the characters in this film move into the Mexican landscape, the less they can rely on communication technologies to "solve" the absurd. No music can drown out their isolation. No device can plug them into a world revealed to be a fraud.

Diegues infuses *Bye Bye Brazil* with a *Breathless*-like curiosity about the life and work going around the main characters and events. This is in pointed contrast to the American road pictures of Hope and Crosby in which the bumbling duo visited Brazil yet saw nothing of it. Brazil, like all of Latin America for so long, was backdrop exotica for Hollywood. In contrast, Diegues presents Brazilian small town life to be full of community spirit and folk wisdom that resists and then integrates the forces of progress to its own end.

Cuarón is equally curious. Luisa exclaims to the boys, "Mexico is teeming with life". Indeed. As the boys joust with Luisa in a small town restaurant, the camera leaves them to follow an old woman walking into the kitchen. She stops in an adjacent nook, downs a jigger of firewater and does an impromptu soft shoe number to a ranchero playing on the jukebox. Then onward to the kitchen itself where a group of women are joyously cooking. Earlier, at the society wedding, the camera tracks with waiters and maids as they deliver food to bodyguards minding the limos idling out in the parking lot.

This film was made shortly before the 9/11 tragedy, a moment that put paid to "The End of History" as it was pronounced by various neo-con/neo-liberal theorists at the fall of the Berlin Wall a decade before. The much ballyhooed Clinton/Blair "third way" of government—driven by policies that were socially liberal, fiscally conservative—proved wanting. The film constantly makes mocking reference to the sclerotic ruling party of Mexico, the PRI, a symbol of everything the third way was meant to obliterate: cronyism, social inequality and that particular supercilious sense of *noblesse oblige* that middling bureaucrats exude when they gain use of a chauffeured limousine. And yet, the current government of Vincente Fox has stumbled and the PRI are still a force to be reckoned with in Mexican politics.

As is often the case, the fantasies of a faster, more mobile (AKA better) world are no match for the realities of the world in its present state. People are so busy marching forward that they can't smell the shit on their shoes. The Oaxacan countryside is not only chronically underdeveloped; it resists development. The police are everywhere, hassling *campesinos* while the boys blithely worry about getting caught with their stash. The countryside confounds the fetish of progress, so crucial to the globalization project. Luisa feels a deep kinship with Dona Lucia, an old woman she meets at a roadside flea market precisely because the old woman has happily stayed put. The small stuffed animal we see hanging from the station wagon's rear mirror, the narrator remarks, once belonged to the old woman's granddaughter who died trying to cross illegally into the United States. The mirage is not worth it.

Nor, it would seem, is the beach. Exhausted after duking it out with Tenoch while convincing Luisa not to abandon the journey, Julio turns down a dirt road and promptly mires the car in a sand divot. The next morning, Luisa awakes and discovers that they have arrived at a beach as deserted as it is beautiful. She walks in a knowing daze towards the water and wades in, lost to the ecstasy of the moment. One might expect Julio and Tenoch to mend fences. Luisa is now off limits. She has also debased them of the notion that their girlfriends are being faithful to them. But they keep their distance from one another, even when a local fisherman offers to take them on his fishing boat to an idyllic beach miraculously called Heaven's Mouth.

The narrator tells us that Chuy, the jovial fisherman, will lose his boat to a tourism consortium from Acapulco and in two years he will be forced to work as a janitor in a resort hotel. The noble savage will be in chains and his idyll overrun with refugees from the city. The boys are the first conquerors of this paradise, even if that conquest was a bullshit improvisation. Hundreds of beaches around the world have been colonized by intrepid libidos and then further colonized by larger interests. The leisure industries of the global economy need the beach desperately. It functions as a psychic escape hatch, promising a primal connection with nature mitigated by the creature comforts of consumer culture. *Tambien* clearly delights in Barthes's idea that the history is often naturalized, unhappily so; to know about the fate of Chuy diminishes our pleasure watching the boys and Luisa enjoying sun and surf. Their lack of a sense of privilege and their self-involvement are elemental to a larger political problem of the global leisure industries.

Tambien cuts against the clichés of the "coming of age" genre to suggest that the characters are not only changed by their experience, they are ruined by it. Many psychoanalytic screeds are sure to be written about the final night that Julio and Tenoch spend with Luisa in a beach cantina, throwing back beers and egging each other on to more and more outlandish confessions of sexual transgression, including Julio's shag of Tenoch's new age socialite mother. The trio retire to a cabana where a heavy threesome ensues. The next morning the boys wake up almost in each other's arms. Deeply hung over from shame and booze, Julio and Tenoch gingerly prepare to return home. Luisa is going to stay behind to tour more of the beaches with Chuy and his family. She wins? They lose?

An epilogue follows. Almost a year later, Tenoch and Julio meet by chance on the street. The narrator intimates that they have retreated into their own worlds, circumscribed by class and material resources. One is at university, the other at community college. Each are dating girls from their neighborhoods. Over a very awkward cup of coffee, Tenoch reveals what the director has hinted at throughout the film—Luisa was dying and expired a month after the trip, that glorious body they so desired riddled with cancer. Clearly Tenoch and Julio have no idea what to do with this information. Its voodoo qualities are overpowering. Death is out there, circling in the water beyond the safety net of adolescence. The film ends with Tenoch excusing himself to meet his new girlfriend. Julio, left alone in a massive sunblasted diner, chokes on his words as he asks for the check. The ground has finally fallen out from beneath him. Everything is up for grabs.

The film has a happy ending after all.

LIBERATION AND ITS DISCONTENTS

The cinema of exhaustion

by Patricia Ducey

In the midst of the orgy, a man whispers into a woman's ear: 'What are you doing after the orgy'? —Jean Baudraillard

It's 1972 and a suburban couple giggles in line waiting nervously to see *Deep Throat*, the first mainstream pornographic movie. Today, they would proba- bly be surfing the cyberoptic Porn World in the privacy and isolation of their computer cubicles, along with millions of others. A hundred years ago, movie enthusiasts walked miles to nickelodeons to catch a glimpse of new entertainment. Today, movies are relentlessly accessible on multiplex screens and cell phones from Dallas to Delhi, on time-defeating TVs, DVRs and VCRs. Jets, automobiles, optical cable, and 24-hour satellite television flood the zone with images and information. Speed, sex, and liberation: this revolution will be televised *and* digitized, interactive and eternal, wait- ing only for the touch of a fingertip to say 'yes'.

But for all the professed personal, sexual and political liberation we enjoy these days, a certain enervation seems to have crept back into our filmic vocabulary. Modernity, post-modernity, or the end of history: whatever we call our era, the possibilities are limitless. Yet it doesn't seem to be quite enough. *Deep Throat,* for instance, would cause hardly a ripple at the box office today, while *Roman Holiday*, a 60-year-old story of chaste princesses and rascally but good men, remains one of the top grossing videos world- wide. Like Baudrillard's bored orgiast, we seem to be asking: is that all there is?

How does film deal with a rejection of boundaries in real life while still pro- viding a narrative with suspense, continuity and enough meaning, to put "butts in the seats"? Perhaps liberation and repression need each other—at least in the movies—because rebellion does need something to rebel against. Film narrative usually starts with a rupture of established order— an illicit love affair or murder, for example—and then the story arcs to its resolution. But this trajectory dangles precariously from the cliff of morali- ty, which would prove unsatisfactory to modern audiences. Must the affair end, is the murderer truly guilty? Today's filmmakers must redefine tradi- tional storytelling for our "after the orgy" or "end of history" era.

Phantom of the Opera, for instance, modernizes the original 1890 tale (and even its stage version) by adding a bookend prologue and epilogue that places the narrative firmly in post-exhaustion territory. The films opens over a gray, post-World War I Paris, thus hinting that the excess the Phantom embodies, the frenzy of *fin-de-siecle* Paris itself, invites apocalyptic destruction. The film ends at Christine's tomb, the inscription of "beloved wife and mother" on her tombstone, as her husband leaves a talisman of the Phantom at her grave, in a last gesture of understanding and love, affirming the redemptive power of traditional morality and the rightness of her earlier painful choice. The world has been destroyed by Thanatos; Eros rescues it, albeit temporarily.

Sideways, however, retreats somewhat from the cliff's dizzy edge. Miles is a true anti-hero, rebelling against convention and morality entirely. He rejects success by working as a high school teacher—teaching English Lit is portrayed as pointless drudgery—and refuses to finish his novel; he steals money from his mother and lies to his best friend, all without narrative explanation or rationale or punishment. Only Jack, as comic foil to Miles, is punished for wrongdoing, as we see vividly when the woman he has lied to and seduced a week before his wedding beats him to a pulp. But what to do about act three, a "resolution" to the predicament of these two lugheads? Insert Maya, the beautiful, wise and caring goddess, who, in a bit of *deus ex machina*, becomes attracted to Miles. We then see him through her eyes (and the demands of traditional narrative) as a lost soul worth saving. In her speech about wine and its connection to those who create it, she reasserts the social bond Miles daily shreds. Whether Miles hears her message, or can possibly live up to it, provides much needed energy to the rest of the story.

Open Water, however, subverts traditional narrative to explore modernity and exhaustion quite successfully. Writer/director Chris Kentis uses several subtle narrative techniques to deliver a masterful unity of narrative, aesthetics and philosophy.

Susan and Daniel, *Open Water's* protagonists, embark on a deep-sea scuba diving vacation to scratch the itch implicit in their placid existence. Perhaps a *frisson* of danger will alleviate their "stress": an energizing whiff of death, then a quick jet plane home.

The opening sequence in the released film is a tight shot of the waves rushing onto the beach at sand level, the natural level of the sea and its denizens, then a quick cut to the couple's large, well furnished home. Inside, Susan and Daniel are each tethered to cell phones and computers and even talk to each other via cells, although they're only 10 feet apart. Thus armed with their communication paraphernalia and bags full of intricate, expensive gear, they head for the islands.

The DVD offers an opening sequence that Kentis later cut. The same tight shot lingers at the sea instead of cutting to the couple's home. Flies swarm an object on the beach—until a hungry tern swishes the flies away and we see a close-up, we don't realize it is a dead and decaying fish. The sea then coughs up more dead things: two empty and torn scuba jackets. Kentis—wisely, I think—drops this opening and builds the character of a threatening nature in more subtle ways; by not telegraphing the ending, he adds to its power. He lets nature begin its assault slowly. After we see their land life, the irritations on vacation become ominous clues: the hotel room's air conditioner is broken and they're grousing, uncomfortable; a buzzing fly keeps them awake all night as Daniel helplessly flails away trying to kill it; an unseen insect or insects burrow into their vitamin pills while they sleep. Nature intrudes an inch at a time; violence lurks just beneath their illusion of civilization and they cannot see it. The film asks, is technology helping them or crippling them?

The film places Susan in the discourse of modern gender equality, as well. Their normal milieu, that of the harried business executive, is gender free. She frets over business issues with a colleague over her cell phone while she moves through their large and comfortable home. Obviously, she has helped purchase it. Some critics have remarked this sequence of the film is badly written and so ordinary that it's boring—but "boring" is the point. This new opening sequence illustrates the shallowness, posing as mastery, of their lives and serves to highlight their incompetence later. In fact, Susan and Daniel seem to reverse traditional gender roles. She is perhaps even more allied with the sphere of work than he is. In another deleted scene in the vacation hotel, Daniel implores Susan to get off the phone—he's been waiting an hour. She brushes him off; he cuts off her call. Susan bursts into rage and slaps him. They're both shocked at the violence of her reaction. Away from "civilization," aggression reasserts itself. "I don't know what came over me," she says, truly surprised and sorry, but they both laugh it off. Sex, too, is a negotiation. In the hotel room, Susan demurs, "not in the mood," in a rejection of a traditional romantic coupling, and turns away from Daniel.

Once on the dive boat, they half listen to the guide who tells his paying customers not to worry about the sharks. In his sanitized version of nature, sharks don't really attack humans—besides, frightening the customers is not good for business. Underwater, they pet the sea life and snap more pictures. They thoughtlessly meander and, once they surface, are surprised that the boat is gone. Slowly their sense of security begins to crumble.

They see a shark far off and Daniel unsheathes his knife; however, Susan mocks his bravado, as Kentis subverts this cue to the traditional "heroic" narrative.

The background music and photography now subtly change. The happy island reggae gives way to a somber bass note thrumming in the background, denoting danger and suspense. The folk tunes slow to keening spirituals. The entire movie frame is sea and sea alone, moving, shimmering—and laughing at the tiny humans it has ensnared.

At the midpoint of the film, after hours in the sea, Susan begins to sob. Daniel takes her by the shoulders and vows, "I know this sucks, but we're going to get through this!" In a more traditional narrative, a speech such as this at the midpoint signals that the protagonist will now gather his strength and intellect and defeat the enemy. And, so, we follow the story trustingly. But as the sun sets on their first day in the ocean, the sun and sea turn blood red. A foreshadowing? The sharks circle ominously, as night falls. A lightning storm erupts. As the thunder and lightning drown out their pathetic screams, we wonder how the hero is going to get them through this. Perhaps Susan, the woman warrior, is the hero instead?

The next morning, however, the sun rises over a peaceful sea, but Daniel is dead. Kentis has snatched the promise of heroic denouement from underneath us. We watch helplessly as Susan kisses his lifeless face and pushes his body away. She stares blankly as the sharks pull his body under. The camera lingers on her calm visage—she is beyond struggle now, the destruction of illusion complete. At that final moment of illumination, Susan finally sees and tastes and feels the true nature of existence. The camera shoots the final scene in a long shot. We watch as a small figure in a wide-open sea slips out of her vest, the only remaining accoutrement of her techno-life, and plunges herself down into the sea. The bass thrumming stops—the story from the human POV is over. Whether serving herself up in a Dionysian embrace with the sea and shark, or merely escaping a more hideous death, she at once becomes tragic and heroic: she sees her fate, the ultimate fate of all, and embraces it.

The screen goes to blackout. The ending credits then roll over a montage of laughing vacationers. A dockhand lugs a captured shark up onto a table, pries open its fierce and bloodstained jaw, and slits open the stomach. Out pops Daniel's ever present camera. Nature is food, nature is death—and so the worm turns.

Every age imagines itself as modernity, conquering the injustices, fears and stupidities of the preceding age—just before despairing of its own failures and excesses, that is. Film genres wear themselves out as well and reinvent themselves later for new audiences. *Open Water*, especially, ably melds the filmic and philosophic for today's freewheeling but world weary zeitgeist.

THIS MACHINE KILLS FASCISTS

Why sub-culture no longer exists

by Nicholas Rombes

"Real life is becoming indistinguishable from the movies." - Horkheimer and Adorno, "The Culture Industry" (1944)

"Where are our real bodies?" - eXistenZ (1999)

THIS MACHINE KILLS FASCISTS. So said the lettering on Woodie Guthrie's guitar. What links that statement with Hermann Goering's that "every time I hear the word culture I reach for my pistol" is their shared recognition of the raw power of culture: it can kill, and it can make you want to kill.

I lost a Canadian friend last week over an argument about *Vanilla Sky*. "It may not be a good film, but it helps me generate a theory," he said. I called it rotten nonetheless, and he thought I was calling him rotten by implication, and that was that. I don't think he wanted to kill me exactly, but there was one moment there.

Critic Robert Ray once wrote of the avant-garde that "nothing is easier than the provocation of a riot by a putative art statement. . . All you have to do is lead an audience to expect one thing and give it something else." Which is exactly the reason a film like *Vanilla Sky* crashes and burns so beautifully: it tells you what to expect, then gives it to you in large, unambiguous doses, a kind of roving, rubber-lipped pedagogue who can't wait to tell you what you already know, what you have known all your life.

The frantic replication of reality on TV shows and in movies desperately and unsuccessfully masks the truth that the real is running out—it's practically all used up. We recoil at movies like *Vanilla Sky* because they take this central Horror and transform it into beautiful math: Tom Cruise's deformed face or Penelope Cruz's collagen lips—the film equates them both in order to ensure the same administered experience for the ugly and beautiful alike. There is no moment of doubt, no sideways look, no hesitation in the dirge-like progression of the film that might give audiences a chance to enter into it in a way of their own choosing. "Here is how you are supposed to feel," the film says, and then tries very, very hard to make you feel that way. Cameron Crowe has said that *Vanilla Sky* is "a movie to think about and talk about later—that idea was built into it."

Does this sort of self-consciousness and manipulation signal the end to the kind of vulnerability that marked the best films of the post-punk film movement, films like *Donnie Darko, Ghost World, eXistenZ, Memento, Mulholland Drive, Tape, Gummo, Fight Club, Requiem for a Dream, Time Code*, and *Being John Malkovich*? While these films operated at the forefront of change, anticipating and giving visual and narrative shape to thornier cultural undercurrents, films like *Vanilla Sky* make orthodoxy out of every radical idea, draining them of danger and fitting them into patterns that are safe and familiar. A movie like *Vanilla Sky* offers a reproduction not of the illusion of reality, but of the very mechanisms of that illusion—it's a crummy movie because it tells us what we already know, and then proceeds to show it to us again.

While history has shown us that film movements burn out and give way to more sober, official versions of a culture's irrational fantasies, there is a difference today, and that difference has to do with how films live on archived on DVD. Which is to say: DVDs are much more than simple information storage and retrieval devices—they represent a whole new shift in the relationship between films and viewers.

Take the new Special Edition DVD of Christopher Nolan's film *Memento*. Judging from some of the reaction you'd think everyone who'd seen it was reaching for their pistols. Sure, the DVD has its defenders (there's always somebody who will defend anything) but overall the reaction has been closer to outright hostility. "It's infuriating, it's monotonous, and it's not worth [the money] for the aggravation," is one of the typical hostile user comments on amazon.com.

In case you haven't seen it, the DVD comes packaged as a psychiatric report "in the matter of an application for the admission of Leonard Shelby an allegedly sick person," complete with a plastic paperclip holding together a sheaf of papers, including a medical history and a portion of a police department report which is actually a brief set of directions for how to play the movie (there are no directions, or menu for that matter, for how to access the supplementary features). It emerges from the same ethos that sprung Mark Danielewski's novel *House of Leaves* or Ben Marcus's book *Notable American Women* or music by the *Yeah Yeah Yeah's*, where you never know if it's serious or even if it's real. To get the movie to play in a rearranged chronological order, you need to find a panel of illustrations showing a woman with a flat tire and arrange the actions in reverse sequence.

This requires some time, to be sure, but its subversive gesture is in acknowledging that the arrangement of information in any narrative is matter of strategy and choice, a process normally denied the viewer when watching a film. What began as experiments in Stanley Kubrick's 1956 film *The Killing* or in the cut-up method as practiced by William S. Burroughs in his writing are now part of the logic of almost every new DVD, which allows viewers to reconstruct a movie in blocks, or chapters. This puts the responsibility for the creation of meaning more squarely on the shoulders of the viewer: depending on which of the many deleted scenes I choose to watch on, say, the *Donnie Darko* DVD, and in what order I choose to watch them, my experience and understanding of the film is likely to be much different than yours. In fact, it's not only possible but likely that you and I won't even ever watch the same "version" of the film; it's democracy verging on anarchy.

In this sense, the chapter structure of DVDs is simply an extension of an old movie trick—the flashback and flash forward, those rare moments in classical Hollywood films where the invisible style of editing (which beautifully disguised the wild temporal and spatial jumps of any film) lost its transparency and became apparent to the audience. The chapter structures of DVDs are extended versions of the flashbacks and forwards, except that today the viewer has a tremendous degree of control over when and where to insert these temporal dislocations.

Playing off the idea of an incomplete archive, the packaging on the *Memento* Special Edition is suitable for a medium that is itself archival (the DVD with its multitude of supplementary features), and especially for a movie whose subject is the unstable archive of memory. If the postmodernists delighted in the demolition of the bogus boundary between reality and illusion, then this DVD never assumed there was one: there is no "real" menu to fall back on, no safe reminder that it's just a hoax. It reveals a movie for what it always is at its best: an elaborate, intimate game between the audience and the film itself. Rather than lessening the power of illusion, it stages it on a whole other level. A good, risky DVD experience reminds you of all the choices available to you in the best films, such as: which characters will you identify with in the film and are these the same characters the film wants you to identify with? *Memento* withholds the answer to this question as its central thesis and then goes from there.

It is the condition of our time the speed at which the notorious, the shocking, the surprising become routine and commonplace and we become bored. *Blair Witch*. *The Osbourne Show*. Cloning. *Donnie Darko*. We barely had time to appreciate their strangeness before they were replicated and we became cynics, the first to say, "that was no big deal after all." This pretty much eliminates the possibility of a subculture: there is simply no time for an underground identity to develop before it finds its way into the mainstream. Speed itself becomes the new value: content is merely the parasite that rides the speed beast. The very rapid-fire process of incorporation of the radical into the norm all but obliterates differences between marginal and mainstream; after all, what is the mainstream today other than an amalgamation of modified subcultures?

The DVD format is ideally suited to this fact, as its very technology gives us the possibility of choice (options, bonus materials, menus), so that in addition to the selection among films, we also have available selection within a film-the power to rearrange the story in a sequence of our choice. Soon we will also be able to re-edit movies, as well as add or subtract content, delete lines, modify transitions between scenes, even cut in scenes from other movies (this is already happening on the internet). The new art will be one of pastiche, where the notion of dominant authorship—the auteur theory—is truly dead. This was predicted back in 1968 by Roland Barthes, who wrote that "the removal of the Author . . . is not merely an historical fact or an act of writing; it utterly transforms the modern text," and that "the birth of the reader must be at the cost of the death of the Author."

Which is why *Memento*—even in its crazy Special Edition DVD format—makes so much sense, and why *Vanilla Sky* is an anachronism. Audiences already know that the real was used up a long time ago, that the Author is dead, and that what we're left with is inventive rearranging, a game that *Memento* knows how to play with savage humor, both in the film itself and in its exploitation of the DVD apparatus.

On the *Memento* DVD—and on others like *Donnie Darko*—the film itself is lost, an afterthought. And isn't that the savage attraction of movies like *Memento* in the first place, the secret knowledge that we are aliens, most of all to ourselves? Who is this man? Who is this nation? What war is this? So what if I can't find my way around the DVD—even if I could navigate it, I couldn't remember how I did it. What was it I was searching for? Okay, there is Leonard, doing it again, forever.

The post-punk film spirit lives on, even after the movement has ended, embodied in DVD archives that remind us that even though the real was shattered long ago, there is still much fun to be had in messing with the pieces.

Like Leonard, I'm an imposter. I'm free of history, roaming a fragmented-world. I have been liberated. So have you.

KILL BILL UNPLUGGED

How reshaping reality may haunt us yet

by Nicholas Rombes

Compared to Pulp Fiction, *which managed to shape old material into new cinema forms, he's [Tarantino] faithfully devoted himself to recreating scenes from his favorite trash films frame-by-frame. —Tomohiro Machiyama*

The remix and the original. The copy and the doppelganger. Who is who in a theater of sounds where any sound can be you? —DJ Spooky

The *Kill Bill* films, with their relentless sampling of international movie traditions—ranging from French New Wave to Hong Kong kung fu, to Japanese samurai, to Italian spaghetti western—showcase an extreme form of filmmaking that openly acknowledges that art is a mix of other texts and styles. When so many films today proceed as if encumbered in an elaborate and tangled harness, what to make of the raw confidence and pleasure of *Kill Bill?* Tarantino recognizes this secret truth: all movies are rip-offs of something else. They all borrow, beg, and steal. They are an amalgamation, a mix, a sampling of others. When Marshall McLuhan wrote that "the medium is the message," he was recognizing this simple truth that all stories are basically recirculated stories, that it is merely the process and technology of telling that changes. Tarantino openly acknowledges this, and in some ways the *Kill Bill* films are fine examples of pastiche, which according to theorist Fredric Jameson entails "the cannibalization of all the styles of the past, the play of random stylistic allusion." For Jameson and other post-marxist critics writing in the 1980s and 90s, this pastiche—which is different from parody because it does not share parody's subversive humor—is symptomatic of the sickness of postmodernism, which rummages through history and culture and in the process defangs it and makes it into just another commodity.

What *Kill Bill* does is reveal this raw process of sampling, a process whose gestures and metaphors have for some time been associated with music (sampling, mixing, peer to peer, file-sharing, etc.) but have for too long been unacknowledged when it comes to film. For it is true that some films are remakes, but all films are remakes of reality. They all steal shots of the given world; they all sample reality. And if there's anything to lament about CGI and other processes of creating highly controlled alternate realities, it is that these forms of special effects foreclose the possibility of the sheer accident and chaos of reality. (This point is driven home in the bonus features of computer animated features like *Monsters Inc.*, where the outtakes only serve to create nostalgia for the real and remind us that of course there are no outtakes as there is nothing accidental in the film.) If *Kill Bill* steals from other movies, it does so in the same way that you or I steal from reality when we open our eyes.

In a conversation with Matthew Shipp, theorist musician Dj Spooky said that "Well, no one owns language. Language is language. Period. And permutation is what makes it all happen. It's nice to have a sense of humor about origin, since there is no real beginning, middle or end." This notion is further developed in the brilliant new book by Dj Spooky, *Rhythm Science* (MIT Press, 2004), where he writes that today's "notion of creativity and originality are configured by velocity: it is a blur, a constellation of styles, a knowledge and pleasure in the play of surfaces, a rejection of history as objective force in favor of subjective interpretations of its residue, a relish for copies and repetition." Or, put more succinctly, today's artist is like the Dj, for whom "the selection of sound becomes narrative."

Kill Bill's relentless mixing of other film styles, traditions, and genres is testament to this logic of mixing, which values creativity not so much in the invention of new stories (impossible) but rather in the selection, arrangement, and modification of existing stories and images. It's not that *Kill Bill* is the first pastiche movie, but rather perhaps that it so unabashedly acknowledges its status as a mix film. More significantly, *Kill Bill* does not need to be read as irony or parody or homage for it to work; without apology it samples, rearranges, and makes something new. In so doing it recognizes that it is in the arrangement of pre-existing texts that new texts are created, and that the new auteur director is akin to a Dj, mixing together existing samples to create difference.

It is difficult today to talk solely about content in any meaningful way: whether a film is pro this or pro that, whether it is too violent or not violent enough, whether or not it endorses the correct worldview. It's not that content no longer matters, but rather that film consumers are increasingly involved in shaping the narratives they consume. Meaning is just another special effect. It is as easily dissected as a camera shot or a CGI sequence. Whether it be clicking through the internet, or managing and arranging downloaded and swapped songs, or manipulating the sequence of a film on DVD, or making and editing their own, or choosing characters, perspectives, and attributes in video games, film viewers are increasingly involved in the creation and arrangement of stories. Read in this light, the *Kill Bill* is not about anything other than its own status as a hijacker of other films, which were themselves hijackers of other texts. And we are all hijackers of reality.

In many ways last year's *Masked and Anonymous* (2003) is a companion piece to *Kill Bill*: both are films that operate openly on the level of theory, both are concerned with the use to which old forms can be put. *Masked and Anonymous* owes less to other movies than to the tradition of Roland Barthes and Walter Benjamin, especially his posthumously published *Arcades Project*, a labyrinthine, fragmented collection of notes, observations, and aphorisms about departments stores, advertising, photography, Marx, railways, world exhibitions, to name just a few. Always threatening to spin out of control, the *Arcades* (written on and off during the 1920s and 30s) is a collision of quotations and commentaries that is a product of the alienating tendencies of capitalism that it sought to critique. Apart from all that *Arcades* is a fun and dangerous read, and one that—in its hypertextual, fragmented style—offers premonitions of our current mix culture.

It's perhaps no surprise that *Masked and Anonymous* was so vehemently rejected on all sides: Dylan purists hated seeing their god shuffling around the movie on a human level, while those who always disliked Dylan anyway saw it as further evidence of his hypocritical detachment from the very System that has made his fame possible. But the movie will surely outlast these easy dismissals and grow in fame as a testament to the possibility of downright strangeness in an era when there is so little patience for the obscure and oblique. This isn't to say that *Masked and Anonymous* is some cheap art-house excuse for poor storytelling, but rather that, like the *Kill Bill* films, it's an experimental film. It is a movie whose dialogue is almost entirely aphoristic, proverbial. In the tradition of Walter Benjamin, Roland Barthes, Theodor Adorno, and Greil Marcus, the writing in *Masked and Anonymous* recognizes that truth lies in the in-between moments, the pauses between lines, the collision of ideas and utterances. Here is a random sampling of lines spoken in the film by various characters:

• *[Human beings] build hospitals as shrines for the diseases they create.*

• *They're all religious wars.*

• *No one is virtually free. You're either free or you're not free.*

• *Everybody's doing the killing now. Everybody's doing the dying.*

• *Happiness can't be pursued.*

• *When you come right down to it, there are only two races: workers and bosses.*

• *People are impressed by people who win things.*

• *One sad cry of pity. In a town without pity.*

• *Keeping people from being free is big business.*

Both *Kill Bill* and *Masked and Anonymous* are further evidence that the old distinctions between *avant garde* and mainstream cinema no longer have any meaning today. Everyone is an *auteur,* and there is no unified media system against which an *avant garde* might define itself. *Masked and Anonymous'* experimentalism—its rejection of proscriptive dialogue in favor of aphorism and ambiguity—reminds us that experimental work can emerge from the most unexpected of places. In this way, too, the *Kill Bill* films and *Masked and Anonymous* are companion pieces: the radical pastiche and flattening of history in *Kill Bill* is balanced by the strong political dimension of *Masked and Anonymous*, which offers a horrifying portrait of a possible America, or even an America which is already emerging.

Dear reader, our dark question is this: what will be the payback for our voracious pillaging and reworking of reality? The mix culture that Dj Spooky describes in *Rhythm Science* is a potentially utopian one. "Play with the recognizability of texts and see what happens," he writes. And yet, we live with the perpetual knowledge that, as it has always been, the real might very well strike back and lay waste to our appropriations. Reality is the ultimate remixer. In David Cronenberg's film *eXistenZ*, the revolutionary Realist played by Jude Law confronts the virtual reality game designer at the end of the film. Before shooting him dead he asks him: "Don't you think the world's greatest game artist ought to be punished for the most effective deforming of reality?" A film like *Kill Bill*—with its relentless mixing of texts which themselves are third or fourth generation remixes of previous texts—reveals to us a new level in the deformation of a reality which shall not remain forever subjugated.

WHAT LIBERAL MEDIA?

by Eric Alterman

Given the success of *Fox News, The Wall Street Journal, The Washington Times, New York Post, American Spectator, Weekly Standard, New York Sun, National Review, Commentary* and so on, no sensible person can dispute the existence of a "conservative media." The reader might be surprised to learn that neither do I quarrel with the notion of a "liberal media." It is tiny and profoundly underfunded compared to its conservative counterpart, but it does exist. As a columnist for *The Nation* and an independent Weblogger for MSNBC.com, I work in the middle of it, and so do many of my friends. And guess what? It's filled with right-wingers. Unlike most of the publications named above, liberals, for some reason, feel compelled to include the views of the other guy on a regular basis in just the fashion that conservatives abhor.

Take a tour from a native: *New York* magazine, in the heart of liberal country, chose as its sole national correspondent the right-wing talk-show host Tucker Carlson. During the 1990s, *The New Yorker*—the bible of sophisticated urban liberalism—chose as its Washington correspondents the Clinton/Gore hater Michael Kelly and the soft, DLC neo-conservative Joe Klein. At least half of the "liberal *New Republic*" is actually a rabidly neo-conservative magazine, and has been edited in recent years by the very same Michael Kelly, as well as the conservative liberal hater Andrew Sullivan. Its rival on the "left," *The Nation*, happily published the free-floating liberal hater Christopher Hitchens until he chose to resign, and also invites Alexander Cockburn to attack liberals with morbid predictability. *The Atlantic Monthly*—a main stay of Boston liberalism—even chose the apoplectic Kelly as its editor, who then proceeded to add a bunch of *The Weekly Standard* writers plus Christopher Hitchens to *Atlantic's* anti-liberal stable.

What is the hysterically funny but decidedly reactionary P. J. O'Rourke doing in both *The Atlantic Monthly* and the liberal *Rolling Stone*? Why does liberal *Vanity Fair* choose to publish a hagiographic Annie Liebowitz portfolio of Bush administration officials designed, apparently, to invoke notions of Greek and Roman gods? Why does the liberal *New York Observer* alternate *National Review's* Richard Brookheiser with the Joe McCarthy-admiring columnist, Nicholas von Hoffman—both of whom appear alongside editorials that occasionally mimic the same positions taken downtown by the editors of *The Wall Street Journal*. On the Web, the tabloid-style liberal Web site Salon gives free reign to the McCarthyite impulses of both Andrew Sullivan and David Horowitz. The neoliberal *Slate* also regularly publishes both Sullivan and Christopher Caldwell of *The Weekly Standard* and has even opened its pixels to such conservative evildoers as Charles Murray and Elliott Abrams. (The reader should know I am not objecting to the inclusion of conservatives in the genuinely liberal component of the media. In fact, I welcome them. I'd just like to see some reciprocity on the other side.)

Move over to the mainstream publications and broadcasts often labeled "liberal" and you see how ridiculous the notion of liberal dominance becomes. The liberal *New York Times* op-ed page features the work of the unreconstructed Nixonite William Safire and for years accompanied him with the firebreathing—if difficult to understand—neocon A. M. Rosenthal. Current denizen Bill Keller also writes regularly from a soft, DLC neoconservative perspective. Why was then-editorial page editor, now executive editor, Howell Raines one of Bill Clinton's most vocal adversaries during his entire presidency? Why is this alleged bastion of liberalism, on the very morning I wrote these words, offering words of praise and encouragement to George W. Bush and John Ashcroft for invoking the hated Taft-Hartley legislation on behalf of shipping companies, following a lock-out of their West Coast workers? (Has *The Wall Street Journal's* editorial page ever, in its entire history, taken the side of American workers in a labor dispute?) It would later endorse for re-election the state's Republican governor, George Pataki, over his capable, if unexciting, liberal Democratic African-American opponent, Carl McCall.

The *Washington Post's* editorial page, which is considered less liberal than the *Times* but liberal nevertheless, is just swarming with conservatives, from Mr. Kelly to George Will to Robert Novak to Charles Krauthammer, among many more. On the morning before I finally let go of the draft manuscript of this book, the paper's lead editorial is endorsing the president's plan for a "preemptive" war against Iraq. The op-ed page was hardly less abashed in its hawkishness. A careful study by Michael Massing published in *The Nation* found, "Collectively, its editorials, columns and op-eds have served mainly to reinforce, amplify and promote the administration's case for regime change. And, as the house organ for America's political class, the paper has helped push the debate in the administration's favor.

If you wish to include *CNN* on your list of liberal media—I don't, but many conservatives do—then you had better find a way to explain the near ubiquitous presence of the attack dog Robert Novak, along with those of neocon virtuecrat William Bennett, *National Review's* Kate O'Beirne and Jonah Goldberg, *The Weekly Standard's* David Brooks, and Tucker Carlson. This is to say nothing of the fact that among CNN's most frequent guests are Ann

Coulter and the anti-American telepreacher Pat Robertson. Care to include ABC News? Again, I don't but, if you wish, how do you deal with the fact that the only ideological commentator on its Sunday interview show is the hardline conservative George Will? Or how about the fact that its only explicitly ideological reporter is the deeply journalistically challenged conservative crusader John Stossel? How to explain the entire career of Cokie Roberts, who never met a liberal to whom she could not condescend? What about *Time* and *Newsweek*? In the former, we have Mr. Krauthammer holding forth and in the latter Mr. Will.

I could go on almost indefinitely here, but the point is clear. Conservatives are extremely well represented in every facet of the media. The correlative point here is that even the genuine liberal media is not so liberal. And it is no match—either in size, ferocity, or commitment for the massive conservative media structure that, more than ever, determines the shape and scope of our political agenda.

HUMANISM ON THE ROPES

Media in the age of terror

by Don Thompson

Humanism has been getting a bad rap lately. After relentless hammering by the religious right, who determined sometime after World War II that "secular humanism" and the United Nations were forming a unholy alliance to undermine the moral fabric of the globe, humanist values are definitely on the wane. In this long-standing cultural argument, it seems that the religious right may be winning. Humanists, particularly in the United States, are on the run or in retreat, and this reflects in many camps, not the least of which is media and film. Increasingly conservative media commentators can seemingly bowl over anybody with their aggressive demeanor and strong beliefs, particularly wimpy liberal humanistic nice guys who question the veracity of such things as the war against Iraq. Combine this with a cable TV centric youth culture (at least the one created by adult-owned corporate media such as MTV) that seems bent on embracing cynically motivated "extreme" non-values—well that spells trouble for humanists. One of the last bastions of mainstream media humanism, Disney, has even gotten so cynical that its most compelling protagonists are Toys or Monsters. Both *Toy Story* and *Monsters, Inc.* got it right—the real monsters are the consumer crazed kids.

Everyone in the US seems to finally be getting on the same page: what matters is strength and power, and the weak will get pushed aside in the natural order of things. *Blade II* and *Survivor,* with their strong over the weak message, have taken front and center as the icons of modern US pop culture. More often, the weak are the humanists, or maybe in the case of *Blade,* humanist vampires. The conservatives and the cynics, well, they're all the new men of action, and with G. W. Bush as their front guy, they get all the media play nowadays, protecting us from "unforeseen events that may or may not occur."

The co-opting by the right of the media can best be seen in the total lack of any representation of true leftists. The "anti globalization" types don't even make the radar screen (although you do see token images of anti-war protesters once in awhile), while G. Gordon Liddy shows up on CNN Money Line pitching his book about how we're losing our civil liberties to gun laws. By the way, I'm sure G. Gordon's appeal is quite broad. Along with Bible-toting Deer Hunters, a lot of atheistic skinheads, whether of the urban or rural kind, must love G. Gordon.

In short, combine enough jaded cynics with enough pious conservatives, and value-based humanistic normalcy gets squeezed out by a media smelling a ratings bonanza in a new world order based on a combination of aggressive conservatism and corporate-driven (and youth targeted) nihilism. The only faintly humanistic sentiments one will encounter in prime time are from advertisements that promote how corporate globalism is creating one happy human family (but some of those companies, like Global Crossing, are defunct so don't do that anymore). Feelings of human connectedness we used to get from positive message films like *Field of Dreams* can only be found in commercials for IBM. But what about counter culture? What used to be considered "counter culture" has morphed into "extreme" and is now so co-opted by the marketing machine of US entertainment conglomerates so much that what was once contrarian is now conformist. To be decadently hip and cool is in fact normal, and Howard Stern is no longer a rebel, but the pioneer of the new nihilist elite. Moreover, hipness is often associated with violence, rooted in hyper-violent video games such as *Grand Theft Auto* and films like *The Fast and The Furious* and *XXX*. Thus the new "counter culture" fuels the youth hungry military machine in stead of rebelling against it, and George Patton is smiling down on us from heaven. And if you're looking for Ozzie and Harriet, well they're long gone, except on Nickelodeon. Witness the newly "normal" Ozzie—that is of the Osborne variety.

As far as the religious right, they've got their own TV and movies (*Jonah: A Veggie Tale*) and books (*The Resurrectionists*) and gated communities in Colorado and Texas, and can just shut everything out with Internet filters and V-chips. They apparently do come out of hiding in droves on election day, while humanists grouse about how "they don't make a difference" and apparently decide to stay at home on election day and watch *West Wing* instead. The religious right has basically given up on secular media and entertainment. In fact, religious types love the newly degenerate main-stream, as it proves their point that the country is going to hell and must be saved by ever more right leaning politics (with the war on terror, many in the middle are becoming scared into following them). And since degener-acy-as-entertainment seems to sell nowadays, corporations are raking in the cash, so everybody's happy.

But what is this humanism stuff anyway? Simply put, humanism has at its core a belief that human beings all have an essential value, and that evil doesn't exist *per se*, but only in evil actions based on hatred. Thus hatred becomes the true evil, not people. Moreover, we must choose not to hate. Humanism is based on the belief that love and human connections must be proactively supported and created through human effort in education, the arts, human centered government policy, and reaching out to find common ground.

Now doesn't that all sound very radical, weak, horrible, and well, humanistic? Well, it's considered *normal* in Europe. But not so according to almost everyone you talk to in the US where such center to left leanings can label you patently un-patriotic. Ironically, as the right wing keeps the government out of such things the culture business, Hollywood steps in to fill the gap based on market economics, or worse, corporate non-values masking as the market. Want to thank somebody for stupid films, TV and music that emphasizes mindless violence, shallow sex and cardboard characters: thank your local conservative who keeps government large and small from investing in "non commercial" artists who might create an alternative to buck this trend. We talk about 100,000 cops on the street and Homeland Security, how about 1000 humanistic independent low budget digital films to provide the fuel for cultural health and offer the world an alternative view of our sensation-obsessed American culture? But no, we prefer the market, a "reality" often skewed by corporate exigencies, and these so-called market forces often lead us to the least common denominator, not risk taking creative vision. And the more conservatives try to rid us of media ills through fundamentalist moralizing, the worse it gets. Take Monica Lewinski: the conservatives go after Clinton for sex, and create a sexual revolution in the media as a result. Once the semen stained Blue Dress hit NBC news, it was all over. The result is *Extreme Dating* and the *Anna Nichole Show*.

In the new media order, stimulation replaces feeling, and heroes and villains become the only acceptable moral guideposts.

Heroes and villains. On daytime talk shows, people try to show how they are "right" or they've been "wronged." Heroes and villains, and their corollaries, winners and losers and of course—victims. In films, in foreign policy, in the crime dramas, in law suit insanity, in the gross out comedies, in the news, because the media (fiction and non-fiction alike) wants to tell good stories and good stories are always based on heroes and villains. The result is that entertainment and reality blur. Will the War on Terror morph into the ultimate reality series? It makes sense: according to the *Village Voice*, the US military funded the prototypes of many of what became the ultra violent video games.

Now there are of course still examples of humanism in film and media, but they continue to wane. What are those examples? For one, *Dead Man Walking*, a film that forgives the murderer and sees in his eyes human value, and the value of love. Or Kenneth Lonnergan's *You Can Count On Me*, a film that shows the subtleness of human interaction in a way that informs and enlightens our own lives. Or, believe it or not, *40 Days and 40 Nights*, a film that posits the value of connection as paramount over sex for sex's sake and displays the potential for a comedic mainstream film to lean toward the humanistic. As for television, much of the programming on PBS is another example (although Bill Moyer's has been under fire lately). If you want to check out classic films that define humanism, take a look at *High and Low*, Kurosawa's masterpiece that forces the central character to face his tormenter, and realize that the tormenter is in fact the tormented. Or *Bicycle Thief*, De Sica's impassioned plea for social justice that rose out of the rubble of World War II.

Disturbing as it might be to many, some of the most humanistic films of the decade have come from one of our bitter enemies and member of the "axis of evil": Iran. *A Time for Drunken Horses, Children of Heaven, The Color of Paradise*. How is it that such a patently "evil" country such as Iran can deliver to us such sweet notions of simple humanity in the face of poverty and suffering? It is because, for one, these societies still suffer on a basic level, and understand they can't deny suffering as some kind of perennial disease to be drugged into non-existence either through television or Prozac. Suffering is, as they Buddhist's say, the first noble truth. It is through staying in touch with that essential fact that we stay in touch with our humanity. In seeking to eliminate suffering with an answer wholly mate- rial, Americans can also eliminate love and compassion, which can rise from that suffering, and may in fact be the key to suffering's true cure.

And still, we are a great nation, and capable of much good—and perhaps even a renaissance of humanism. At least I want to believe that, although it becomes harder for me to believe that all the time.

If voices of humanistic balance do not rise in greater numbers, I fear for our country and our future. We will likely not win the long term war on terror- ism (will it last forever?), because we are quickly losing the moral authority to win any war, at any time. Certainly not pre-emptive wars that skirt inter- national law. In the short term we may win battles, but the long-term war will be lost, primarily by our own hand. We may have lost it already.

CHIMES AT MIDNIGHT

Revisiting the Shakespearian Welles

by Mike Shen

INTERVIEWER: What is your major vice?

ORSON WELLES: Accidia—the medieval Latin word for melancholy, and sloth... I have most of the accepted sins—envy, perhaps, the least of all. And pride...

INTERVIEWER: Do you consider gluttony a bad vice?

There must have been good feelings, and good wine, flowing in the hotel room where that interview took place, for Welles took no offense at the question. "It certainly shows on me," he admitted. "But I feel that gluttony must be a good deal less deadly than some of the other sins. Because it's affirmative, isn't it? At least it celebrates some of the good things of life."

Welles was in London; it was 1966, and he was acting in the James Bond film *Casino Royale*. He was about to unveil *Chimes at Midnight*, his film adaptation of Shakespeare's Falstaff plays, at Cannes. A quarter-century had passed since Welles, as a limber twenty-six year old, had made *Citizen Kane*; he had put on the fat that he would wear for the rest of his life, and, purely on physique, made a magnificent Falstaff. Life, too, had given him insight into Shakespeare's most popular rogue. "The truth of Falstaff," he would later observe, "is that Shakespeare understood him better than the other great characters he created, because Falstaff was obliged to sing for his supper." Falstaff was cherished for his wit but scorned for his decadence; Welles was celebrated as a genius even as he struggled to finance his films, accused of frittering his talent, and, more deadly to his career, of squandering studio money. As Falstaff, Welles offered his rebuttal on-screen:

CHIEF JUSTICE: Your means are very slender, and your waste is great.

FALSTAFF: I would it were otherwise; I would my means were greater, and my waist slenderer.

Boasting an excellent cast, including John Gielgud as Henry IV and Margaret Rutherford as the addled Mistress Quickly, *Chimes at Midnight* nonetheless belongs to Welles; here, as in *Touch of Evil*, the director makes inspired fun of his own face, exaggerating, with wide-angle lens, the Santa Claus jowls, the inflamed, merry bulb of a nose. He carries his bulk with wonderful grace, sprinkling the performance with minute, almost imperceptible bits of physical comedy—a hand on the gut, a wobbling of the knees, a quick ballooning of the cheeks. But the accidia comes in handy too, as Welles explores the tragic side of Falstaff, the impoverished, disease-ridden loser who, in Shakespeare, doesn't even get to die on the stage.

In creating *Chimes at Midnight*, Welles stitched together pieces of five plays—*Richard II, Henry IV 1 and 2, Henry V,* and *The Merry Wives of Windsor*—to tell the story of Falstaff's friendship with Prince Hal, and of the prince's eventual rejection of his companion. The film shakes up the chronology of the plays; conversations that begin in *The Merry Wives of Windsor* finish up in *2 Henry IV*, characters pop up in the wrong places, and two battle scenes merge into one.

"Naturally, I'm going to offend the kind of Shakespeare lover whose main concern is the sacredness of the text," Welles told an interviewer. "But with people who are willing to concede that movies are a separate art form, I have some hopes of success." In the plays, Hal's morality is ambiguous; his betrayal of Falstaff is a necessary means to restore honor to the crown and stability to the realm. But Welles glosses over the political dimensions of the plays, preferring to emphasize the human story of Falstaff's betrayal. Practically all of *Henry V,* in which Hal conquers France in five acts, is squeezed into a single, ironic line of voiceover: as the narrator extols the greatness of the new king, we cut to Falstaff's rowdy tavern crew, rolling away an enormous casket. Falstaff, of course, has died, for "the king has killed his heart."

The words may be Shakespeare, but the aesthetic—fast-moving, oblique, deliriously off-balance—is unmistakably Welles, and the eight-minute battle sequence, a whirl of galloping hooves, whizzing arrows, and broken heads, is among the greatest in film history. The blocking is deft, the camera placements unexpected and precise; yet at the same time, there is something profoundly unfussy about Welles's style. There's plenty of room left, in those famous deep spaces, for the best dialogue ever written.

"You always overstress the value of images," Welles once told a critic. "Only the literary mind can help the movies out of that cul-de-sac into which they have been driven..." Only a formalist of Welles's standing could get away with such heresy. For movie buffs, literary adaptation is a red flag. (Think of Joel McCrea in *Sullivan's Travels,* as the misguided Hollywood director who wants to make a pretentious lit-film called *O Brother, Where Art Thou?*). It touches on our deepest fear, that cinema is still poor cousin among the arts. Remembering Orson Welles—the man behind *Chimes at Midnight*, Othello, *The Magnificent Ambersons*—should help us to rest a little easier at night.

AN INTERVIEW WITH ROB NILSSON

Cannes, Sundance, and life with Cassavetes

by Don Thompson

Thompson: How did you first get involved with filmmaking?

Nilsson: I got an idea that wasn't a poem, a painting or a song. I had avoided filmmaking because my grandfather did it. But I got hooked. It was in Nigeria. I made a film with some friends called *The Lesson*. It was an adventure, a lark. It was also about neo-colonialist stereotypes. Tarzan, Kurtz, and Dr. Schmutzer were all there. Luckily for film history the only copy was stolen.

Thompson: I know Cassavetes was a big influence on you. Did you ever meet him? Any interesting stories about Cassavetes?

Nilsson: I knew John for several years. I met him at the Chicago Film Festival the year *Northern Lights* played there. When I made *Signal 7* and dedicated it to him, he called me up. "Rob, I loved your film—I loved it and Gena (Gena Rowlands, his wife) loved it too and we never agree about anything." That was the best compliment I ever got. When I sent him *Heat and Sunlight*, he called again. "Rob, Rob, I saw your film and... and... I can't talk right now." This didn't sound promising. Then the phone rang again. It was Gena in a very calm, firm voice. "Rob, this is Gena. John saw your film and he liked it very much."

Toward the end of John's life, when he was very sick, we'd get in his old Lincoln and drive through the Valley. He told me all of the war stories about making the movies which had given me my original inspiration to be a filmmaker. He used to tell me I should never have dedicated a film to him. "Rob, it makes it difficult for me to praise you. Everybody thinks it's just self interest."

Thompson: You won the Camera D'Or at Cannes for Northern Lights. *How did that project evolve? What was it like at Cannes during those days?*

Nilsson: Northern Lights started out as a 30 minute documentary financed by the North Dakota Committee for the Humanities and Public Issues. But John Hanson and I started shooting dramatic scenes. We presented a sprawling mix of the two. The Humanities Committee was either completely impressed or totally confused. At any rate they could see we were on to something. "Now about that 30 minute documentary..." they said. "Let's finish that and then we'll talk about a dramatic feature." John Hanson was a master diplomat and that's how *Prairie Fire* was born and how *Northern Lights* got its start. I believe if we had gone to them originally proposing a dramatic feature film, *Northern Lights* never would have happened. We won the Camera d'Or at Cannes for *Northern Lights* in 1979, the same year *Apocalypse Now* and *The Tin Drum* tied for the Palm d'Or. I thought it was a good start.

Now Cannes is certainly a place on the make. In the long run, however, it's misleading. You have to follow your instincts no matter what the world says. If they close the door on you, you must work in your own idiom. Likewise if you are the world's darling. Everything changes, including your work. But the work has to change out of a determination to explore your personal unknown. Cannes chose *Northern Lights* to praise that year. But they were just some people sitting in a room. Who were they? And *Northern Lights* is not my favorite film. I'm more interested in what I'm doing now, or will be doing tomorrow.

Thompson: Heat and Sunlight *won the Grand Jury Prize at Sundance early on in the festival's history. What was that experience like and how has Sundance changed?*

Nilsson: It's nice to win awards. But the work is the real thing. We danced around when we won. We thought we deserved it. But tomorrow the fascination begins again. You scratch your itches. You want to see how the thing will look. So you make it. As for Sundance, it has become a sort of Wal Mart or Home Depot for low/middle brow taste. The good? Sometimes films like *Irreversible* play there. The bad? The rest of the film school training wheel cinema they play there. How could it be different? There is almost no independent American Cinema worth watching today, and Sundance exists to present it.

Thompson: *You sometimes work with a script, sometimes not. What's the difference in how you approach a scripted and/or non-scripted film. Do you feel either method is inherently better than another?*

Nilsson: A scripted piece is filled with obligations... and goals. You try to service your expectations. This is a dangerous path requiring special skills, including the skill of forgetting. In other words, you rehearse and think out what you're going to do in advance. And then you must proceed as if you don't know what you're doing in order to keep the characters honest and fresh. That's a tough balancing act. When you don't have a script, but have spent weeks on back story improv, where characters get used to being in their fictional skins, you bet that you will find unplanned miracles from relaxed, concentrated performers mining the moment. And often times you fail. But film is not a real time medium. Failure can be turned to success in the editing room—which is really where a film is made anyway. In the Circus: Oh. Oh. the character fell off the tightrope. End of show. But in the cinema you cut to the audience. And when you cut back, the acrobat does a double flip and lands on his feet. Personally I prefer a sense of complete truth to the moment, and a more general truth about what feels real, plausible, rooted, inevitable. If that's not there... I couldn't care less.

Most scripted stuff creates a proscenium reality. In other words, let's block off the streets, put up the yellow tape and keep the riff raff out. I want the riff raff in. I want all the human messiness to be there... or I want to feel it could be there, that it's included in the filmmaker's mind. That the bottom line of being alive is never neglected.

Thompson: How do you keep actors emotionally honest?

Nilsson: Hopefully they already are honest. Hopefully they haven't been destroyed by the degraded work the film business gives them to do. Hopefully honesty is what they want, because if they don't, they wouldn't want to work with me. That's what I'm trying to be, to do, to promote honesty... maybe the only thing. Luckily I have a workshop I go to every Wednesday night in The Tenderloin (San Francisco). There we test each other. Workshop members attempt to mine honest inspiration and I try to recognize it, encourage it, find ways to engender it. We need to practice this relationship because it's hard to get it right. How could that be? Is truth that rare a commodity? Well, when you add up fear, ambition, self interest, and the competing claims of children, lovers, parents, families, fellow artists and business connections, your sense of reality can be stretched rather thin. But if there's one place where the only thing valued is total human presence in the here and now and a completely honest and open soul to explore it, maybe you have a better chance of finding it.

Thompson: How did you begin to work with the homeless in San Francisco? How has that experience shaped your life artistically and personally?

Nilsson: My brother had been missing for many years and I got interested in the brown baggers, the shopping cart ladies, the screamers, the shell shocked, the rogue elephants with their monickers and fellowship of the damned. And who were the people who wanted to be alone for their own reasons? I found no answers to those questions. I found individuals with very interesting lives, thoughts, hopes. I found pain and suffering, delusion and inspiration alike. I found people with talent but little opportunity. So I created the Tenderloin Action Group, now the Tenderloin YGroup, and 13 years later I'm still interested. Of course, by now, the group has taken on its own identity and now fewer people come directly from the streets. It's an all comers workshop about human expressivity. We have professional actors, people from all walks of life hopefully more healthy, saner, and more motivated for their work in our circle. But we're in the Tenderloin, meeting at the Faithful Fools Ministry, open to anyone interested in our searches.

Thompson: *You call your technique "direct action." What do you mean by that?*

Nilsson: Direct Cinema is a term coined, I believe, by the Maysles Brothers for a kind of documentary where life is allowed to happen in front of Cameras, and a shape and meaning discovered in editing. I turned that insight toward fictional drama and added the word "action." Direct Action has a political meaning. It emphasizes doing rather than talking. "Action" is also the director's traditional starting gun. It's more complicated than that so interested people should go up on my website, www.robnilsson.com, to read the Direct Action manifesto.

Thompson: *Your recent film* Chalk *has won wide acclaim. Was* Chalk *a significant turning point for you in terms of how you made films?*

Nilsson: *Chalk* was the first film I made with the Tenderloin Group but I had been working with the techniques and ideas for Direct Action since *Northern Lights.* Perhaps the first real Direct Action film was *Signal 7,* which we shot in 1983. But *Chalk* was unique in that it was the first film made with my on-going street ensemble, the Tenderloin YGroup. Don Bajema and I did write a script for *Chalk,* but I both used it and put it aside from scene to scene. Since that time I have not written traditional scripts for the personal films I've made.

Thompson: *Your recent* Nine@Night *films have gotten a lot of attention, with the latest in the series,* Attitude, *opening recently in New York. What are your goals with* Nine@Night?

Nilsson: I'm really waiting for the day when we can show all 9 films back to back and se what the experience will be like. All the films interact in non-programmatic ways. Serendipity, 6 degrees of separation, and sheer coincidence are factors in the way characters encounter each other. But I'm also interested in how things go on at the same time and we don't see the connections. That's what *Time Code* was about. What connections seem pivotal and which incidental? What will we know about people seen from different perspectives and viewpoints through the prism of 9 films? I'm eager to find out.

Thompson: *What about technology? What impact does it have, for good or for ill, on filmmaking?*

Nilsson: Without video technology I wouldn't have been able to make the films I've made. I would have been forced to take a more traditional approach to the dramatic feature. The technology would have been too expensive to work with an ensemble of unknown actors on projects which come from personal curiosity. I've also found that digital technology is perfect for the collaboration of circumstantial acting and the editing room. Easy control of the Magicianship of editing makes all the difference.

Thompson: *Since SolPix is often visited by writers interested in film—who are some of your favorite writers? Do you have any favorite translations from literature/plays to film?*

Nilsson: I believe that the richest language of film is more akin to poetry than theatre. I also believe that most people are unaware of what ties images together and creates potential for meaning, suggestion, surmise. They simply aren't educated to know what they're watching. Pictures as metaphors, symbols and meaning devices are what interest me (and the shallow posing of *Matrix Reloaded* is the farthest from what I mean). The simple linear screenplay with its predictable rationality is over for me. The cinema has a long way to go but not in its present form. MTV showed people capable of making profound connections between varieties of images and linking them to human thought and feeling. Filmmakers such as Chris Cunningham, Gaspar Noe, and Mike Figgis attempt to carry those connections into the longer narrative form. This is where the epic poetry of cinema will synthesize with the insights of science and the longings of lyric expression.

Oh, you said writers? For language read Walt Whitman, Emerson's "On Self Reliance", Melville, Gary Snyder, Robinson Jeffers. These are great American poets which show how to live deeply, seeking the boundaries of the human imagination in our native idiom.

MOORE CONTROVERSY

One rambling critic tackles another

by T.B. Meek

When it came to the handling of Michael Moore's acerbic documentary, *Fahrenheit 9/11*, the conservative powers at Disney (which owns Miramax, the production company behind the film) weren't too astute. If they were trying to snuff it from distribution, then why did they sell it back to Harvey and Bob Weinstein? You knew the co-founders of Miramax would find a distributor—and they did, through longtime ally, Lions Gate. Plus, by creating a maelstrom of controversy when they dug in their heels and said they wouldn't release the Bush bashing polemic, Disney forever conjoined itself to the film. Any effort to distance themselves backlashed and all but assured box-office success. In its opening week alone, *Fahrenheit 9/11* raked in over twenty million dollars and was the number one grossing film, making it the first documentary ever to score the top spot (which it did on 800 plus screens; the runner up, *White Chicks* was available for viewing on 2,400 plus screens). That same week, Disney released the slight, feel-good documentary *America's Heart and Soul*. Whatever they'd hoped to gain by the gesture (the film didn't even earn a paltry $200,000 in the opening week), it's clear that the lessons learned in the wake of Mel Gibson's *The Passion of the Christ* brouhaha hadn't sunk in at Mickey and Co.

The marriage between Miramax and Disney (which made the acquisition in the mid 90s) has always been an odd duck. From a business perspective, it makes perfect sense; a *Kill Bill* movie costs about half of what it takes to cook a Jerry Bruckheimer-produced film (take *Gone in 60 Seconds* or *Enemy of the State*) and yet nets as much, if not more—less cash up front, greater ROI. Not to mention that since 1994, when *Pulp Fiction* crashed the Oscar party, Miramax has been a perennial force, if not dynasty, at the annual Hollywood awards pageant (*Chicago*, *Shakespeare in Love*, *The English Patient* and so on). Conceptually however, Miramax staples like hit man Vincent Vega or Billy Bob Thorton's *Bad Santa* don't quite fit the image of clean family fun that Mickey, Snow White and Donald have come to represent (though Disney is no stranger to odd ties; one of its tentacles owns the radio channel that controversial right-wing talkmeister Rush Limbaugh employs as a bully pulpit). And while I'm not certain where Disney head, Michael Eisner's political allegiances lie, it is intriguing to note that the mega conglomerate's big dollar theme park is located in Florida, which is governed by the brother of Moore's target, Jeb Bush. Ironically (or poetically depending on what side you come down on) much of Moore's pot-stirring spectacle, which took top honors at this year's Cannes Film Festival, keeps winding it's way back to the Sunshine State. It opens there with a quick recap of Election 2000, deriding Jeb and the Republican Party for hijacking the presidency and later, hangs on a bewildered Dubya as he's informed of the attacks on the World Trade Towers while visiting a Florida elementary school.

Moore's never been the meticulous documentarian that D.A. Pennebaker, Frederick Wiseman or Errol Morris are; he's more of cinematic pundit who employs shock and droll wit to hammer home his points. Forget about laying out facts in a stepwise fashion or building a convincing argument. A typical Moore tactic is to launch a salvo of incendiary images, purposefully juxtaposed to evoke on a visceral level. Take Bush sitting stupefied and inept as he learns of the attacks, then lounging slovenly in a golf cart, and most damning, as he smugly addresses an audience of affluence as his "base." The mélange hits with biting accuracy, but does that make Moore an ingenious stalwart of leftwing liberalism or a shameless manipulator of the Bush blooper reel? Truth be told, he's a pinch of both, but he's got to watch it; his self-aggrandizing demagoguery nearly capsizes *Fahrenheit 9/11* (long gone is the earnest journalist who made *Roger & Me*), and by pursuing Bush with such pit-bull virulence, he subverts journalistic objectivity and threatens the overall credibility of his mission. And then there are the cheap shots. The guitar riff from Eric Clapton's *Cocaine* incessantly demonizing Bush's alleged youthful transgression and during the "seven minutes" at the elementary school, Moore adds an unnecessary voice-over as if he's the voice of Dubya. "Who screwed me?" he says in his scruffy, everyman's twang. The point he's trying to make (that Bush was only thinking of himself and not his country) is abstruse and worse, it's cavil and nearly as smug as Bush as he hangs at the fete's podium, basking in glow of his "base." That said, nothing in *Fahrenheit 9/11* tops Moore's pathetic assault on an Alzheimer's addled Charelton Heston in (the otherwise brilliant) *Bowling for Columbine*, which still remains his all-time low.

The most poignant moments in *Fahrenheit 9/11* come when Moore yields the screen to others. The interview snippets from servicemen in Iraq initially illustrate young, naïve instruments of the Bush administration, but later, some older, more grizzled soldiers express their disillusionment with their mission and rationale for being there. Moore also scores some comical and wholly affecting moments when he corners several U. S. Congressmen and Senators and solicits them to send their children to the war (Moore previously informs us that the troop base, much like Vietnam, is comprised of those from the lower rungs of the socio-economic ladder and that only one U. S. Legislator has an offspring in the war). And then there's Lila Lipscomb, mother of a G.I. killed in action, shaking with emotion as she reads her son's final letter imploring his family to do whatever possible to get Bush out of the White House. No mater how much Moore leans on her to propel his agenda (he drags her down to Washington to conjure conflict), her anguish and anger remain genuine. Beyond her obvious political value,

Lipscomb also marks a critical checkpoint for Moore. She's a resident of Flint, Michigan, Moore's hometown, which he goes out of his way to reference in all his films (his first film, *Roger & Me*, was about Flint's economic decimation due to the General Motors shutdowns in the 80s). And Moore muscles in the celebrity sound bites too. In *Bowling for Columbine* goth rocker, Marilyn Manson provided some surprisingly astute observations about rock lyrics and gun control, in *Roger & Me*, it was game show host Bob Eubanks serving up the cheesy nostalgia, and in *Fahrenheit 9/11*, a ditzy Britney Spears blindly throws her blondeness behind the president. In short, Moore has found a two-step that appeals to *his* "base" and he sticks with it.

Respectively though, *Fahrenheit 9/11* isn't Moore's most tightly focused effort; it's more akin to the director's penned works (*Stupid White Men* and *Dude Where's My Country*) than *Bowling for Columbine* or *Roger & Me*, which pretty much amounts to a sloppy, yet amiable rant against the establishment. Moore simply wants Bush out of the White House and vehemently asserts his will on the screen. And like his pulp works, *Fahrenheit 9/11* plays any angle it can to take Bush's knees out from under him, be it the Election 2000 controversy, dubious oil ties with the Saudis, the hyperbolic projection of Dubya's inaction during the World Trade Tower attacks or the quagmire known as Iraq.

Bombastic overtones aside, there's no denying *Fahrenheit 9/11's* power to provoke, the begging question however, is: come November, will it have any sway on the 2004 Presidential election? Obviously Moore and the Weinsteins felt strongly enough to make sure it got into theaters before the June handover of Iraq, which one would assume, would also be enough time to sink in before the election. But if Moore really wanted to incite Bush's ejection from the White House, he needed to come up with a smoking gun (the liberal equivalent of WMD) or at least endorse the Bush's opponent in waiting. Yet neither occurs in the film. Much of what's rendered is accusation or a regurgitation of what's known and long been conjectured (the findings by the 9/11 Commission and Senate panel are far more sobering and illuminating). And as far as supporting Bush's opposition goes, Moore threw his weight behind General Wesley Clark, the late Democrat entry who disappeared from the field faster than water on a hot griddle—thankfully though, Moore's not liberal, or impractical enough to jump on the Nader train, not yet any way.

When the election machine finally roars into full swing this fall, *Fahrenheit 9/11* won't tilt the vote to John Kerry. It's a nice idea, but a flash in the pan doesn't change an individual's political ideology that's been fostered and hardened over years. It has, however, served as political smelling salts to the American public. Conservatives have become cemented in their defense of Bush, the pulse of liberals has quickened (outside a local movie theater in Cambridge, Massachusetts throngs of activists have been peppering *Fahrenheit 9/11* filmgoers with various calls to action) and those on the fence will have plenty more to chew on. Perhaps the heightened awareness will yield a greater voter turnout? And when Moore disengages from his Bush-hating mode, he does raise some salient questions about the true weight of a voter's voice, the manner in which governmental policies are executed and poignantly poses the notion that America may in fact be a hegemony dressed up as a democracy. But like most leftwing diatribes critical of the reigning administration, *Fahrenheit 9/11* tosses up a battery of issues and offers few solutions. After the election passes and the box office totals are tallied, two things will be certain: *Fahrenheit 9/11* will go on to become most profitable documentary on record and Moore's whirlwind success will incite a sudden outbreak of people seizing up video cameras, digging through archival footage and emblazoning their socio-political crusades on celluloid (Morgan Spurlock's already got his hands on a hit with *Supersize Me*). And don't feel too bad for the folks at Disney, nor assume a trove for Moore and the Weinsteins; Disney, when they sold the film, stipulated that 60% of the profits had to be earmarked for a charity of their picking. Those charities have yet to be selected, so let's just hope that the people at Mickey and Co. do the right thing and send the till to the families of those who perished on 9/11 and the battlefields of Afghanistan and Iraq.

PEACE AS STYLE

How films talk peace in style and theme

by Don Thompson

With the current war in Iraq, the time is ripe to talk about peace movies. Films about peace, with peace as their central theme, speak to us in times of war, reminding us of alternatives. Peace films speak out against the atrocities of war, to be sure, but sometimes within the context of an over-arching violence that is their stylistic core. Other times peace is embodied in both the style and theme of a particular film. Whether or not stylistically violent or peaceful, these films drive home the issues of war and the nature of peace in a way that provokes us, prods us, changes us. Moreover, some films show us a peaceful style within the context of a violent story. These films, in their own way, comment on violence and the Hollywood style that often supports it.

If popular films have dealt with issues of peace, they have often done so within the context of war films: Oliver Stone's *Platoon*, Francis Coppola's *Apocalypse Now* (both about Vietnam), and Carol Reed's *The Third Man* (the aftermath of WW II) being three primary examples. These films heighten or even satirize the reality of war in order to rail against it, or to critique the unrelenting tendency of war to dehumanize. Both *Platoon* and *Apocalypse* are in a sense cop-outs, however, in that they are addicted to the power of violence as a dramatic device, use it to the utmost, squeeze us emotionally and mentally through the unrelenting presence of it, even while doing so in a way that fundamentally reminds us that violence is dehumanizing. Unlike modern films that glamorize violence, these films use violence as a tool to explore the human face of war. When Kurtz (played by Marlon Brando) drops the de-capitated man's head in the lap of Willard (played by Martin Sheen) at the end of *Apocalypse*, Willard is horrified to the core and shaken by the brutality of the act. Kurtz, who has gone beyond remorse to a pathological sense of numbness, has become both superman and subhuman simultane-ously, having stepped outside the bounds of humanity. Kurtz becomes both the detached father-God of heaven, distributing justice without human con-cern, while at the same time becoming the sub-human, the demon, whose very nature is self-destructive. This Yin-Yang nature of war, and its effect on the human psyche, has been at the heart of the post-modern critiques of the realities of war. In *Platoon*, Charlie Sheen's Taylor and Willem Dafoe's Grodin both struggle to maintain their humanity under very de-humanizing circumstances and stand in contrast against the Kurtz-like Barnes, played by Tom Berenger.

Coppola's version of Kurtz (derived from Conrad's *Heart of Darkness*) is not unlike the character of Harry Lime in *The Third Man*, another dark anti-hero who is very much a product of the system. Both *The Third Man* and *Apocalypse* dealt with their dark anti-heroes in the same way: they were

killed off by "good" men who did not lose their moral bearings in the struggle. In *Apocalypse*, Martin Sheen as Willard played the role of "approved"
executioner, mirroring Joseph Cotton's Holly Martins, who killed Orson
Welles' Harry Lime in *The Third Man*. I'm quite sure Coppola was influenced
by *The Third Man* in writing the end for *Apocalypse*. (Interestingly, Welles
had written an un-produced script of Conrad's *Heart of Darkness* and was
definitely attracted to the persona of Kurtz.) In both cases, Harry Lime and
Kurtz stepped over the bounds of conventional morality, but at the same
time retained enough of their former selves to condone their own destruction by their respective protagonists—the "good men" or better, the "good
American" represented by Willard and Holly Martins. That Brando's Kurtz
reflects on a river in the United States, "filled with the smell of
Gardenias," that was Willard's home state is no accident—the heaven of
America (and by inference the "goodness" of Willard) is contrasted to the
hell of the river (and the "evil" of Kurtz) in South East Asia.

The tendency of American culture to require a pathological warrior to exe-
cute its atrocities, and then to disavow that warrior and ultimately destroy
him, is a ritual of sacrifice played out every day in the Iraq War. However,
today's Holly Martins or Willards are not fictional but very real in the minds
of documentarians like Michael Moore, who with his *Fahrenheit 9/11* is the
foil to our dark heart as personified in the also very real Bush family. Moore
would of course very much like to sacrifice Bush in the electoral sense,
even if Bush did what ultimately a majority of Americans felt needed to be
done—remove Saddam Hussein. In a sense Moore is trying to take the
responsibility of the Kurtzes of the world back to their origins: the leaders
that create them. Again, both *The Third Man* and *Apocalypse* have this
theme as central to their narratives—both Kurtz and Harry Lime are as much
a product of war, a necessity of war if you will, rather than evil *per se*.

In Michael Moore's landscape, the real evil lies at the top, where the Bush
family is cast with a dark and de-humanizing influence. Their minions are in
turn mini-Kurtzes, and in Moore's *Fahrenheit 9/11*, we see these de-human-
ized soldier's face to face, playing their heavy metal music, seeing the
enemy as a video game, reigning fear and terror down upon them with a
devilish delight—much like Kilroy (played by Robert Duval) did in *Apocalypse
Now*. It is not the warrior motivated by the goodness of the cause, but
rather by the adrenaline rush of the kill. This corporate warrior (and I don't
pretend that all of our soldiers in Iraq have this attitude, but commenting
specifically on some of the soldiers seen in Moore's film and also evidenced
in the Abu Graib prison abuse) has a different attitude than warriors of the
past (at least the way they are romanticized). It is as if the empty core of

the rationale for the war in Iraq, as well as in Vietnam, provokes an attitude among the soldiers that must either make them monsters or destroy
them psychologically (there is a large amount of evidence that suggests the
later is happening at a rapid rate).

That *Fahrenheit 9/11*—our more recent version of *Apocalypse Now*—has
moved from a fictional narrative that sacrificed its pathological soldier to
keep the corporate and political sponsors safe, to a new landscape that
traces war back to the leaders and directly challenges them is, in many
ways, remarkable. Hard as it may be to believe to many on the left, it
shows the resilience of an American society which may be beginning to look
inside of itself to find the root causes of its obsession with war, violence
and domination. Moreover, we as a society can now tolerate a gadfly like
Moore without persecuting him. Rather than persecute him, he becomes a
millionaire, much like peace-promoting rock stars became rich during
Vietnam. If Bush wins re-election, it will be interesting to see what happens
to the Michael Moores of our society, and if this tolerance will continue.

While American peace films about war make use of violence to weave their
stories (violence is in fact their *raison d'etre*) other filmmakers take a different route stylistically and thematically when dealing with peace. These
films subvert both the idea of war and the idea of violent filmmaking as a
requirement of the Hollywood studio method. At the core of this violent
filmmaking is violent and quick, "kinetic" editing that moves the narrative
forward in an unrelenting fashion and forces the viewer forward like a run-
away train. This editing style, almost taken to the point of absurdity these
days with *MTV*, advertising and hyper-violent movies, all of which make it
difficult to reflect on an idea or image, and a lot easier to manipulate
somebody to your point of view. It is an ideal style for advertising and for
cable channels like Fox.

Filmmakers interested in subverting this violent and manipulative style may
even do so within the context of genre. Hitchcock is the best example of
this, particular with films such as *Vertigo* or *Rope,* where languid tracking
shots and/or the lack of editing as in *Rope,* protested against the violent
style of Hollywood even as he (Hitchcock) dealt with stories that primarily
focused on mysteries and crime. Hitchcock was very much a stylistic subversive.

The master of anti-Hollywood style is Michelangelo Antonioni. Many of his
earlier films, such as *L'Avventura,* would be impossible for modern audiences to sit through without squirming in anxious pain (they were difficult

enough for audiences in the 1950's and 60's). Antonioni would spend minutes on the spinning of a fan or wind through the trees, such as in *Blow Up*. The heirs to Antonioni are numerous, not the least of which is Theo Angelopolous, with films such as *Ulysses' Gaze* (starring Harvey Keitel), or *Eternity and a Day* (winner of the Palm d'Or at Cannes).

My own experiment in peaceful narrative, *Clouds*, certainly had the influence of Antonioni. In many ways *Clouds* was an anti-Hollywood narrative both in terms of style and the "passive" nature of its male protagonist (as a result men sometimes felt uncomfortable with the film). In terms of big budget Hollywood films, the most remarkable stylistic homage to Antonioni was *Castaway*, whose (general) lack of musical score, long tracking shots of the natural landscape of Tom Hank's island prison made me literally gasp that director Robert Zemekis was able to pull it off. I think Zemekis was able to do so because he recognized the longing many people have for nature, for nature directly expressed and unmediated and unedited, and that it is getting harder and harder for people to find the peace associated with a pure and unmediated experience of natural beauty. People certainly would not generally sit down in front of the Grand Canyon for two hours and watch its colors change: audiences will, however, pay 10 dollars to sit and watch Tom Hanks on an remote Island for two hours, if nothing else because it's Tom Hanks, and not the vagaries of their own mind, they have to deal with.

Films that promote a peaceful style do as much to force us to question our attitudes toward violence as do films that overtly deal with violence and war. Antonioni, not much in vogue today although his influence continues (again, *Castaway* being a good example) was the prime mover (along with Jean Luc Godard) and proponent of the anti-Hollywood style (though Godard for different reasons) whose films often dealt with issues of peace—both inner and outer. Antonioni will in my mind remain the quintessential art film director who confounds audiences and delights cinephiles who love his bravado and courage to buck the easy out of a Hollywood style that traces its roots back to D.W. Griffith and *The Great Train Robbery*.

Peace can be both a stylistic and a thematic force. Peace can be forwarded by the style, and subverted by the story, or vice-verse. Perhaps one day we will again see films that are both films about peace that embody a peaceful style. We don't see much of that today, for our addiction to Hollywood editing and special effects keeps us glued to films that stylistically give us little room to think and very little peace. It seems to me somebody probably likes it that way.

AN INTERVIEW WITH KAYOKO MITSUMATSU

Documentaries, now more than ever

by Michael Neff

Neff: *Kayoko, let's get my profound question out of the way first. How has documentary filmmaking evolved over the past twenty years in terms of content, and relevancy to viewers? Has their been a change in role, or are things fairly status quo?*

Mitsumatsu: I think documentary filmmaking for television has changed drastically over the last two decades. To me, it seems individual story telling has taken a back seat to corporate-driven story telling—but with lower budgets!

My latest experience in the US market was in pitching a documentary series *Lost Islands: Six Islands, Six Intimate Portraits, Six Communities In Jeopardy*. It is a fascinating look at six islands of the world, all whose stories have been forgotten or neglected, but yet are a source from which to look at our world. These include the Bikini (Marshall) and Sapelo (Georgia) islands, among others.

When I took this proposal to US, UK, and Japanese major broadcasters and production companies, they all said, "we would have funded if this was five year ago." Their reaction indicated to me that research-oriented, controversial, minority stories are not that welcome any more.

My good friend and producer of documentaries BBC left that company, as they were shifting from serious big scale documentary to the 'docu-drama' type—low budget entertainment-oriented documentaries. This transition is a shame—I remember the wide variety of documentary programs about Gulf War in England when I lived there a few years ago. I was so impressed with the different approaches and views that BBC supported. While I assume this can still happen at the BBC, I think it is less so.

In the US, I think that cable, the digital explosion and new technology have created more channels, and therefore given chances to a lot of independent, low budget documentary projects. But in many cases, it's on the producer's shoulders to fund the initial research and filming, and this can be a huge burden. The big projects are very limited in both topic and diversity— so someone like a Michael Moore stands out in US with his individual style and themes.

I came to documentary filmmaking in 1984 at NHK (Japan's National Public Broadcaster) as a producer/director, freshly graduated from college in Tokyo. That was the year when NHK started Satellite Broadcasting in Japan.

The net impact was that NHK, then the largest broadcaster in Japan, gained two more extra television channels, totaling four channels.

At that time, NHK produced a lot of personal stories with very individual directorial approaches. In the last twenty years, the company has shifted to more globally-oriented topics in its documentary programs. However, NHK is still very unique in that they still fund many documentary programs reflecting a variety of stories. But the trend is definitely toward less controversial stories.

We will see what the new technology can bring during the next decade, but it is definitely providing more chances for anyone to film with digital technology for less funding. I truly hope to see more variety of views, approaches and stories in the world of television documentary.

Neff: How do you weigh market considerations at this time with your passion for heroic filmmaking?

Mitsumatsu: Based on my experience pitching documentary ideas to US outlets, market considerations are extremely important. Basically will not buy unless the market is considered—unless you are a big name.

As an artist, I personally do not tend to think "commercially"—so often I find my projects less marketable. In these cases, I have to think of some twist to make the idea more "mass" oriented.

As an alternative, I can always find a funding source who supports my projects—and do low-budget independent productions. But this takes a lot of commitment and I'm not always up to it.

Neff: It's obvious that you are a champion for good—a rare and gifted kind of artist. You obviously feel very strongly about the various documentary topics you choose to involve yourself with. So how do you choose?

Mitsumatsu: The films I develop and/or direct have been stories that either move me or disturb me. There is always a sense of "who else will do it, if I don't?"—maybe even an arrogant sense. I have to feel that the film will have a unique story, one I can work on given my personal back ground and my personal interests, and one that if I know nothing about, that I can feel comfortable learning about.

First *They Killed My Father* was a good example. I met a powerful Cambodian Refugee Loung Ung, and heard her speak about her ordeal during the Pol Pot regime. That moved me so much, that I just had to try to make something happen. It took three years for me to pitch to NHK—but it got made at the end. I think it is all about how I am moved with the story that drives me to make a decision—not with the intent of being some kind of hero but simply to share untold and valuable stories with the widest audience possible.

Neff: *I can't recall the name, but I do recall the suffering inherent in that documentary film about the plight of Afghani women under the thumb of the Taliban. That film had a profound effect on many people. Do you feel one proper role of documentary filmmaking should be to right injustice and champion human rights?*

Mitsumatsu: Definitely, I completely believe that it is one of the greatest roles of documentary filmmaking. Part of what inspired me to get into the business was when I lived in Brazil and saw some of the deeper reality behind the festival of Carnival. But Japanese programs were not portraying the true picture of people's spirits, their true humanity.

Visual and audio presentation of all the diverse peoples of the world, communicated in the form of documentary, is an incredibly powerful communication tool. And once powerful documentaries are made, they should find the maximum exposure possible in the world. Documentaries are made to be shared with people on the globe—to be a powerful vehicle to communicate between cultures. My film *First They Killed My Father* has not yet been distributed to other countries outside of Japan and Taiwan, and it should be. But I don't have much say—even though I produced and directed the program I don't own the copyrights—NHK has it all. I certainly learned a lesson there!

Neff: *What kind of freedom did you have while working for NHK in Japan? Were you able to choose your subject matter or were you simply assigned a project?*

Mitsumatsu: I was a producer/director for current affairs and documentary programs in NHK in Japan for seven years, and it was our job to propose projects at least once a month. If I had something I really wanted to do, I just went straight to the producer of that particular program, and we discussed it. It was unbelievably democratic process, and my proposals even as a first year director were approved, funded and made.

Before completing the programs, there were a lot of stages of higher producers supervision, which sometime could be either artistic and creative
intervention or censorship. This was the most exhausting process of all—
finalizing the film—as this is where the corporation's interests would factor
in.

Neff: With regards to First They Killed My Father, *how did you get involved
in that project? Did HarperCollins contact you?*

Mitsumatsu: I described this a little bit prior, but I met the protagonist
Loung Ung, while interviewing Jody Williams for her Nobel Peace Prize for
International Campaign for Landmines in 1996. At that time, Loung was one
of the campaign staff promoting awareness of her native country
Cambodia's tragedy during Pol Pot. I remember she only had a simple, one-
page biography as an introduction. But when I heard her story of survival for
four years under Pol Pot, I just could not believe it and I felt I wanted to
make her story more known. It was at this same time that many high profile
magazines were covering Jody Williams.

I kept contacting with Loung for the next couple of years, and she sent me
her manuscript for her book *First They Killed My Father* (Harper Collins,
2000). Reading more about her story was a truly profound experience and
provided many insights for the documentary.

*Neff: What was it like working on that film? It must have been an
emotional experience.*

Mitsumatsu: Working in this particular film as an independently contracted
Producer/Director was in many ways the experience of a lifetime.

To start, I had a great story—but the budget I had to work with was very,
very small. I found great collaborators: Director of Photography Bob Nesson,
Editors Beth Gallagher and Sal Baldomar to name a few. Lots of people
worked with me within the confines of our stringent budget, as they were
all highly committed and wanted to share this story with the world audience.

As far as being emotional—certainly visiting Cambodia, especially Toul Sleng
Genocide Museum, where only 8 out of approximately 20,000 captured sur-
vived—that was a profoundly emotional experience. I never knew how it was

going to feel to stand and feel the air where so many people were tortured to death, from babies to the elderly.

I also gained an incredible respect for Cambodian people, who despite of this national tragedy, continued to smile and have such zest for life. Those people taught me so much.

Neff: You've worked in so many roles. Would you rather produce or direct?

Mitsumatsu: I think I like everything! When I am commissioned to work on NHK's documentary projects as producer or part director, I liked it. On the other hand, I certainly like to do my own stories as a producer and a director.

But I really like creative team work to make a great story to be told. Currently I am asked to be a producer for different projects, and I like that as well. I do not think I can find all the world's great stories by myself!

Neff: Jyakuchu: Magical Artist of Edo *is an intriguing film. Did you learn anything from the making of that documentary that you didn't know before? How would you compare it to your other films?*

Mitsumatsu: I was involved as an associate producer role for this documentary. I really enjoyed this project, especially as the director (from Japan) took a very different approach. He included a dramatic story telling of Edo Period, which was very well done. As I did not really get involved in directing the film, I cannot really compare with my other projects. But I can say that I learn so much from working in different roles in different projects.

Neff: I'm fascinated and very much want to see Betrayed by the Rising Sun: The Comfort Women of the Imperial Army during World War II. *Is there anything about this subject that came as a surprise to you, anything you can share with us?*

Mitsumatsu: This is one project I would like to make it happen here in US. The topic is very much a taboo in Japan, and the surviving victims are getting very old. As we still continue to have wars and sexual discrimination all over the world, I strongly believe it is important to make this story now.

My first proposal did not have too much commercial appeal due to the lack of US perspective, I was told. So I am working on rewriting this project to be more attractive to US companies..

Neff: *What does the future hold in store for you? What types of projects would you like to take on?*

Mitsumatsu: I hope to make *The Comfort Women* - to produce it here in the US, that is the first goal.

The future is not clear, I just keep doing what I have been doing, and remain open minded so that I will have more stories to work with, good stories of course!

ON DEATH AND TAXIS

The taxi as sacred space

by Timothy Dugdale

At long last, it seems *The Apprentice* is running out of gas. Lord knows it's about time. An hour spent with people aspiring to be Donald Trump is an hour too long. The show takes you through many emotions, none of them pleasant. Relief comes only when the smug vulgarian dispatches his victim of the week. The "winners" sullenly cart their luggage up to the suite; the loser heads outside where a yellow cab waits to spirit them away from a dream deferred, if not denied.

But who is the loser, really? I keep waiting for the person in the back of the cab to look out the window and start smiling. The spell has been broken. And then, once over the George Washington Bridge, they order the cabbie to take them to the nearest bar and they buy a round of drinks for the house. Just like Mick (Paul Hogan) in *Crocodile Dundee*, when he goes for a late-night bar-hop in a cab after spending the evening in the company of the snooty boyfriend of the journalist who has brought the crocodile man to the Big Apple.

Charlie Sheen should never have gotten in the back of the limo with Michael Douglas in *Wall Street*. Once you get a taste for riding in those things, you're toast. You're cut off from the little people, you're cut off from the sounds and smells and annoyances that make living in a big city such an exhilarating and maddening experience. The limo is a prison in disguise— luxury at the expense of living.

At the end of *Sid and Nancy*, after he's done us all a favor and stabbed Chloe Webb at the Chelsea Hotel, Sid Vicious (Gary Oldman) eats a pizza, plays soccer with a bunch of kids and then rides to heaven in a New York yellow cab that has come to pick him up. Junkie punk rockers keep it real, even in death.

Some big cities, though, are hardly Thrillsville. In *Ten*, Abbas Kiarostami offers the viewer very little of Tehran through the windows of a de facto gypsy cab driven by a lovely young divorcee. The terrain that interests him is psychic. The "cabbie" picks up a variety of women and they discuss issues and ideas that would be unthinkable in a society dominated by a male-centered theocracy. The car is a privileged space. There is one interloper, however: the driver's young son who rages against her for divorcing his father. You only have to look at his contorted face and listen to him parroting the party line of pious machismo to know that she made the right decision. Driving is liberation.

Only a fool would eschew a taxi in Las Vegas, America's sin soaked boom-town. The heat, the traffic and the ungodly scale of buildings and human beings clogging the skimpy sidewalks make a taxi a must. The Mormons and the military conspired to create a grid in which a city block is a country mile. Elizabeth Shue takes two cab rides in *Leaving Las Vegas*. One cabbie is a real cretin who delights in the terrible back scuttle she endured from a trio of frat boys anxious to do a hooker. The other is the incomparable Lou Rawls offering her soothing, sage advise about love as only he can. There is no come-on in his voice, only concern.

What would a city be without a few kind hacks? A good cabbie knows all the nooks and crannies of the place, where to go, where not to go. They are paid to look away. Or to look again in the rear-view mirror. They can save your day. Or ruin it. I decided to give Madrid another chance, so I saw *Women on the Verge of a Nervous Breakdown*. Thanks to Aldomovar's kind-hearted faith in coincidence, Carmen Maura gets to ride not once but twice with a very wiggy but very sympathetic cabbie who favors leopard skin seat covers and mambo music. The gents are all shits in the film except for this sweet little man with the towering pompadour and unctuously sentimental demeanor.

In *Night on Earth*, Jim Jarmusch offers the viewer five cab rides in five different cities—LA, NY, Paris, Rome, Helsinki—as odes to favorite directors or actors. Only the sequence in Rome works and works beautifully thanks to Robert Benigni who subjects a priest with a heart condition to an explicit confession of his assignations with a pumpkin, a sheep and a naughty sister-in-law.

But it is New York that is synonymous with the taxi. Manhattan is an island full of busy, ambitious people who need to be somewhere fast. Go-getters from around the world arrive daily to stake their claim, including the guys behind the wheel. You can ride in a hundred different cabs and meet people from a hundred different countries. Here is globalization completely local-ized.

Thirty years ago, New York was a different place. The city was filthy, close to bankruptcy and seething with racial strife. Deep in the bowels of *Taxi Driver*, ex-Marine-turned-psychotic cabbie Travis Bickle (Robert De Niro) commits his first murder. While he's doing a bit of shopping in a bodega, a young black punk comes in and tries to hold the place up. Travis pulls out one of the numerous pistols he's purchased and blows the kid away. Stunned, Travis stands over the body not knowing what to do with himself or the heater. Meanwhile, the bodega owner gleefully goes around the counter and grabs a tire iron that he puts to work on the corpse. Travis escapes to his cab. It's an absolutely riveting scene of savagery, perfectly in keeping with the infernal view of New York circa 1975 conjured up by Martin Scorsese and obscenely lapsed Calvinist, Paul Schrader.

Then with his consummate genius for bi-polar dynamic range, Scorsese cuts to Travis, .44-caliber Magnum in hand, finger on the trigger, watching *American Bandstand* on the telly in his hovel. He is absolutely mesmerized by what he's seeing. Here is an America in which a misanthrope and racist like him can live. Through the blue glow of the screen comes the cocksure pleasure of the kids as they sway to the final verse of what is arguably the finest song Jackson Browne has ever written, the title track from his 1974 breakthrough album, *Late for the Sky*. Not only is the melody achingly beautiful, Browne's voice and lyrics are wistful in the extreme. It's a song you imagine being sung by a young studio executive driving away with tears in eyes from his lady's pad in Malibu, after the final breakup of a romance they began in the Summer of Love, but which has now fallen afoul of the realities of a generational hangover. Growing up sucks, especially with Nixon in the White House.

Earlier in the film, Travis romances Betsy (Cybill Shepherd), a WASPy debutante working for the presidential candidate Travis eventually tries to assassinate. She gives him a record by Kris Kristofferson, whom she describes as "part prophet, part pusher." Like she would know.

Travis is unconvinced and takes her to a Times Square grindhouse to debase her of such idealism. It works. She leaves in disgust. The fuse is lit.

When you think of Scorsese and pop music, you invariably think of his period pieces like *Raging Bull* or *Goodfellas* in which pop songs, particularly doo-wop, at once capture the romanticized outlaw machismo of the characters while articulating their pathos. The Bernard Hermann score of *Taxi Driver* builds a coherent, unifying mood of discord and malaise, perfectly articulating the synchronicity between Travis' interior world and the city's rot. An elegy for a downward spiral through Hades.

In *Taxi Driver*, Scorsese is plugged into the moment. First and foremost, *Taxi Driver* is a bleak essay on fame and anonymity in post-'60s, post-Watergate America. Scorsese is not mocking "Bandstand." To the contrary, it is the charmed planet that Travis wishes he were on, where he's in the arms of a dream girl, where he is somebody other than "God's lonely man."

Clark moved "Bandstand" from Philadelphia to Los Angeles, the land of eternal youth (including his own). But it's also a place of incredible deca- dence, a place full of fallen prom kings and queens who know exactly what Browne is saying. Scorsese makes the psychic linkage between the bloody neon hell of New York and the sunny madness of LA — two infernos bracket- ing a country addicted to illusions and lies. As the last strains of Browne's song fade out, Scorsese cuts to the streets of New York where Palantine, the candidate, is invoking the words of Walt Whitman in a speech that Travis watches with sullen menace from his cab. Alone, lost, he is very much late for the sky.

Los Angeles belongs to the limo, not the cab. You think of Richard Gere bearing flowers and opera as he arrives to whisk reformed hooker Julia Roberts away to his sparkling empire. A pretty ride for a *Pretty Woman*. In *Night on Earth*, Jim Jarmusch would have us believe that a class act like Gena Rowlands would take a cab from the airport, a cab driven by Winona Rider. Hah!

LA is a monster with no heart. The city is spread out enclaves, rich and poor. At night the core is empty. But the conceit of a contract killer hiring a limo for the night to cart him from hit to hit would test even the most pow- erful suspensions of disbelief. How would they converse? Over the intercom? Or perhaps Tom Cruise could ride up front and they could cruise on over to Chateau Marmount and wait for a fellow celebrity Scientologist in need a ride home? Hence Michael Mann, director of *Collateral*, has Jamie Foxx shuttling Tom Cruise around in a cab. I've always thought Mann's best work was in *Thief* because he achieves a superior balance between plot, charac- ter and style. *Collateral* fires strong on two of those cylinders: character and style. Foxx's cabbie is hardly a lifer. He's ready for better things in the music industry but they cost money. So the risk and reward equation of the taxi is a necessity. The film opens with him picking up and chatting up Jada Pinkett-Smith. Better than digging ditches. Where he drops her off, Tom Cruise is waiting. Foxx's night is in the crapper. This is just the sort of thing Mann, the crypto-Buddhist loves: outrageous circumstances for an ordinary guy who has to endure them until he creates a solution. The Big Test. *Collateral* owes more to *Groundhog Day* than it does *Taxi Driver*.

That Foxx will triumph at the end is a given. More complex is the fate of Cruise. He dies on the subway, not in the cab that has long since been destroyed in an escape ploy by Foxx. Earlier, Cruise's hitman mused darkly about a man dying on the subway and being left to ride the line all night, back and forth.

VON TRIER FOR DUMMIES

The non-technique of Dogme

by Don Thompson

Lars von Trier is arguably the greatest cinema auteur (or anti-auteur, if you prefer) of recent times, although many people in the US (outside of Cinophiles) would be hard pressed to know who he is or what he stands for. Even among intellectuals he remains a mystery, confounding as many as he enlightens.

As a relatively recent von Trier observer, and quasi student (though not yet practitioner) of the *Dogme 95* movement (which some believe now to be dead—thus it's probably a good topic to dissect), I felt obligated to give my two cents worth on von Trier and what I think he might be up to. Since SolPix tries to speak to cinema as a cultural event, rather than a mere horse race of box office receipts, von Trier represents an ideal topic for discussion. He is an artist in search of an impact without much concern for box office appeal, or so it would seem.

And yet von Trier cannot be seen outside of the economics of his filmmaking. His move to DV with *Dancer In The Dark* may have been as much out of necessity as of want, and yet the film's theme and technology meld in a unique statement that could not be made outside of the form within which he chooses to speak. Nor can his choice to move the language of his films from Danish to "European" multi-lingual to English be seen outside of a desire to reach out to a wider audience, which is in a sense an economic choice as much as an artistic one. Thematically, there is a continual movement from cynicism to sentiment—or mockery of sentiment—depending on your point of view. Sentiment becomes both an object of longing and an object of scorn, as if what was destroyed must be rebuilt, but it cannot, for it is too late.

The cynical see this movement of von Trier as a copping out—von Trier loses his nerve—and yet the sentiment he postulates is based on real human emotion that is lost in a cynical time where the so-called "cool" have often become enemies to beauty, even as they attempt to redefine what that word means in the name of egalitarianism. von Trier becomes a documentarian of the decline of the West (or evolution of the West, if you like what you see)—the triumph or tragedy of civilization as it either loses its moral compass or shakes off its shackles, but in either case loses its ability to feel.

In the neat, and often unexamined, world of the West created by the sometimes too easy relationship between the cool, the technological, the commercial, the aggressive and the militaristic, our humanity is often compromised, and from this place we often react negatively to von Trier. It is also a world where commodified sentimentality and spirituality, whether that be Disney or the New Age Gurus or the 700 Club, mimics its "secular humanist" consumer-market enemy in order to battle it, and in the course of the battle everyone loses, or maybe everyone wins because they all seem to make money. But still there are real winners and losers, although they are not discussed, for they are not worth our attention. This is the world von Trier critiques. von Trier invites us into his films as if to a place of worship, but with a wink, like Reverend Lovejoy of *The Simpsons*, whose church placard reads, "We Welcome God and His Victims."

I haven't seen all of von Trier's films, but will draw here from *The Element Of Crime*, *Zentropa*, *Breaking The Waves* and *Dancer In The Dark*. *The Element Of Crime* and *Dancer In The Dark* are, respectively, his earliest to his most recent work, with *Zentropa* and *Breaking The Waves* being in the middle, and each representing an ending and a transition, respectively.

As is well known, the idea of *Dogme 95* (aside from giving some people migraines) is to break ties with cinematic formalism and free the director and actors to a kind of cinematic truth. Dogme forces the director, by its very nature, to focus on performance and writing—the raw elements of cinema—and to negate his role as auteur (at least in theory). This is done by allowing only hand held camerawork and limited lighting, among other non or anti-techniques. It's like making a writer hand write a novel, and illustrate it himself, as Blake did when he first self-published his books. It is also similar to Martin Luther's (the original one) dictums of the Protestant movement, with von Trier nailing the Dogme method on the Cathedral door of cinema's stylistic excesses. Interestingly, Dogme has a similar goal to Hollywood's original "seamless" style—that is, to remove the sense of an individual director.

Breaking The Waves was one of the first—if not the first—*Dogme*-like films and also probably the movement's best example of communicating pure emotion. von Trier himself has recently spoke of trying to reach a "direct transmission" of emotion with his films—a term almost religious in its connotation—but given that the technology of filmmaking must, even if stripped to its minimum, stand in the way of this "directness" (and may even call attention to itself) there is a tension between the ideal and the reality. This tension reveals one of the many contradictions inherent in von Trier, contradictions which in themselves become a common thread throughout his films. In his Dogme attempts at anti-style, von Trier remains the consummate stylist.

Prior to *Breaking The Waves*, with films such as *The Element Of Crime* and *Zentropa*, von Trier shows himself a master of both cinema formalism and intellectual rigor, creating landscapes of decline and darkness fueled by a sense of environmental and/or moral collapse. If the crime in *The Element Of Crime* cannot be solved, it's because of the fragmentation of the self which cannot be brought back together again in a future world where technology and industrialization have made the entire landscape toxic. In *Zentropa* (with the European title *Europa*), the relentless train of progress collapses on the bridge, and drowns the protagonist, the naive American Leo (played by Jean-Marc Barr), in the morass of European culture. It is a Europe that von Trier, and America, cannot wrestle free from, that drags American culture back to its base—and apparently corrupt—roots from which it cannot escape.

Ironically, it is a sentimental interpretation of European culture (rather than a view of Europe as corrupt)—a Europe idealized by America and epitomized in films such as *The Sound Of Music*—that von Trier parodies so well in *Dancer In The Dark*. In *Dancer*, the European (Czech immigrant Selma, played by Bjork) in America is destroyed by a system that makes the innocent guilty through a dehumanizing work environment, forcing the protagonist to Dance in the Darkness of meaningless and mindless labor and brutal system that squeezes the sacred out of her experience, and ultimately destroys her as evil, even if she is the emblem of good.

Dancer In The Dark, while sometimes called a diatribe against capital punishment, is really a diatribe against capitalism itself, and the seemingly insane moral reality it can spawn where those that naively celebrate beauty are destroyed in the name of the—as Ken Kesey put it—"the Combine." With von Trier it is in the relationship between the celebrators and life and its oppressors that transcendence becomes the victim's last laugh, as the beautiful rises into magical bells over an oil rig somewhere in the Atlantic, as in *Breaking The Waves*.

In *Dancer*, capitalism as a reality—particularly in its American brand—is portrayed as patently anti-spiritual, anti-life, and anti-beauty. The idealist Selma (as in Selma, Alabama, home of Martin Luther King's sixties civil rights march) brings about her own destruction through an audacious stubbornness to see beauty in everything—to sing in the midst of Capitalism and its factories, and to care more for her son Gene (whose genes may cause hereditary blindness, with which Selma is already afflicted) than for the system that supports (or enslaves) her and will not pay for her family's health care. It is a system, which, rather than value her perspective, kills her as a threat, even as she continues to see a (delusional) beauty through her blindness, a delusion that itself may also be a truth. It is in fact her audacity to continue to believe in the beauty of her oppressors in the midst of corruption that allows her to defy gravity, even in her death. In tandem, the tragedy of Selma is that she continues to see the world through the delusion of *The Sound Of Music* (also an emblem of the "pure" and "seamless" Hollywood film!) rather than face the reality of her oppressors and the truth behind the facade of the American dream.

It is in a similar, Christ-like sacrifice of Bess (played by Emily Watson) in *Breaking The Waves* that reveals human relationships at a more basic level, where the crux of the human question is fundamentally in the relationship between man and woman—not in social relations—in the intimate reality where the blood of woman is continually sacrificed for the life of man. For this reason *Breaking The Waves* may be the purest of von Trier's films, as he takes us to the barren landscapes of Northern Scotland, where there is nothing but raw human relationships left, even if they are supported by the monolith of civilization, symbolized by the oil rig looming in the huge North Sea: a feeble attempt at structure in the infinite.

What better place for transcendence than an oil rig—the source of power for civilization—the emblematic choice that mankind made to fuel his society by the black stuff rather than love, that fork in the road made at some point where mankind determined to remain tied to the soil, to the (according to our mythos) corruption of the Earth, rather than to transcend it. And yet any corruption is only the result of man's attempt to mold, to bend, to control to his own end—to dominate the landscape, earth, woman (as in Bess' sexuality)—to wield these inherently pure elements into objects of power. Thus the powerful manipulate the innocent and attempt to corrupt that very innocence in the name of progress (or greed). The result is a community of the compromised, AKA modern civilization. The Bells at the end of the *Breaking The Waves* propose a transcendence over compromised human existence, but the men remain tied to the rig, to the Earth and its power, to the black ooze that fuels their civilization and from which they cannot escape. They can only look upward to the Bells, and hope to rise toward them in death.

It is Bess' purity which saved her (at least spiritually)—her love—a purity which could not be corrupted by her husband Jan (played by Stellan

Skarsgaard) as he vicariously uses her "perverse" sexuality to gain strength. So it is her purity that finally cures Jan of his paralysis, even as that same purity curses him to worship her, transformed as she is into the pure sound of the bells, from below. Bess is the "Mary/Mary" dichotomy—the Mary Magdalene and Virgin Mary all rolled up into one, as a single voice and a single woman. The Goddess and the Whore, all in single package.

This analysis makes sense in the light of von Trier's (purported) conversion to Catholicism (if you take it seriously, that is). What can be taken seriously is that both a cynical and spiritual interpretation of von Trier's intentions remain valid, simultaneously, in a kind of dialectic that when taken as a whole create the equivalent of an artistic Zen Koan (i.e., a contradiction intended to bring about enlightenment, such as meditating on the phrase "the sound of one hand clapping"). There are other tensions and paradoxes that when brought together into von Trier's narrative whole create an impossibility, a moral and philosophical conundrum, that can only be resolved through the unifying power of love. It may be that for von Trier the only alternative to the morass of *The Element Of Crime*, a future world that von Trier surely wanted to avoid, becomes to eschew an addiction to power and the chronic need to "solve" the crime (or to "direct" a film), and to instead accept life as it is—replete with all of its contradictions and multiplicities of perspectives and truths. Moreover, it's as if by confronting the darkness of his own cynicism in his earlier films, von Trier moves to faith as an answer, but a faith which never wholly dismisses the critical self-reflexivity of postmodernism.

Much of that critical analysis brings him back to the fundamental issue of power. It is in the relationship between an addiction to power and the stubborn (or courageous, if you see it that way) refusal of man to bend to nature and see, in context, the futility of his struggle to finally understand nature (and therefore conquer it)—the relationship between that addiction and to the innocence it both destroys in the name of civilization and longs for once destroyed—that creates the layering of relations that is spilled out onto the screen in von Trier's films. Further, von Trier must finally reflect on the act of filmmaking itself, and the need to forsake the power of the "author" in order to reach the purity of cinematic truth.

If the decline of the West is true, according to von Trier it is because the reality of the West's created moral universe is ours and ours alone, and stands quite separate from natural reality—that we don't admit this truth and that we cling to our fabricated social truths as "givens" of the natural world, when in reality we may in fact be an aberration in the natural world, more akin to a disease on Earth than the pinnacle of evolution. If the decline of the West is true, it is in part due to our inability to look critically, as von Trier does, behind the artifice of human self and admit, with courage, our true state, which perhaps is not as enlightened as we would like to think—but at least from that point could come the possibility of enlightenment. For von Trier seems to posit that in looking inward at that self that we will see not only the often selfish monstrosity that results in our current civilization, but also perhaps something quite different, perhaps something sacred. And from this realization, from this looking and analysis, individual and cultural maturity can begin.

Some American critics dismiss von Trier (particularly more recently with some of the sheer venom that *Dancer* brought about) because they don't have the time for him, frankly, as he has taken too long to develop his philosophy and is too crafty in his presentation. They also fear him because of the realizations—personal or socially—that he might prompt. Certainly a world fueled by the pure love that Bess or Selma demonstrate would be one far different that the one we encounter, and far less controllable by the powers that be.

American directors tend toward the obvious, wearing their philosophy on their sleeve, always revealing the literal "narrative" surface instead of the paradoxical human subtext—and always with formal considerations divorced from theme. In most cases the result is a complete abandonment of humanism, even in the so-called "art" film. With von Trier, form and theme are always one thing and cannot be separated. For this reason he is an artist. American directors feel quite comfortable with formal cleverness that isn't grounded in philosophical struggle—perhaps because American culture tends to see that struggle as a sign of weakness; that we feel our American view is a given and should not be questioned; that we equate the powerful with the good; and that we feel (at least based on what we aspire to) there is something inherently superior in the successfully (usually wealthy) clever amoralist when compared to the reflective (and usually poor) idealist. Further, the protagonists in von Trier's films refuse to hate the enemy, to choose a villain and overcome it—but rather seek connections between people. For this reason he is a humanist, or at least a humanist in progress.

American directors have, for the most part, abandoned a brief flirtation with humanism (the so-called "golden era" of American filmmaking in the 70's and, by extension, the "independent" movement as represented by directors such as John Sayles) and settled back into genre and spectacle—revealing themselves as hack technicians at worst and at best, competent architects in service to a larger animal, AKA, the marketplace. From the American viewpoint, since all philosophy has been had, there can be no new ground to break. It's all ultimately about good and evil, and not the common ground human beings share. Moreover, since the Earth has become toxic and corrupted, there can be no purity in nature to inspire great art. They may be right, for the toxic landscape itself has become the inspiration for many a post modern filmmaker.

With *Breaking The Waves* von Trier recognizes that the purity comes back to the human, often to the form of the woman, whose body and sexuality may be the last bastion of natural beauty in a polluted world, and thus explains the continued worship of her image in church and in storefront windows. The Dogme technique forces von Trier back to the raw human elements: the face, the body, the gesture, the look. It forces one to question the techniques that form "cinematic language" and seen as "givens" by most directors. It is the antithesis to the trend toward special effects and of what I'd call hyper technique—that is, to continually move away from the human in an attempt to "move the medium forward" toward some heightened sense of a reality, when in truth human experience is where reality was all the time. We aren't unlike Dorothy in Oz, and von Trier is our Wizard reminding us to tap our shoes three times, that truth lies not in escaping into something inhuman, but in facing the mirror of self, and shattering it.

But instead we listen to another Wizard, who wows us with spectacle and technique. Our American cinema so often takes us down the path of spectacle perhaps because at heart we are ashamed of sins both known and unknown, and must hide in a creation somehow inhuman or superhuman (is there a difference?) to escape in a reality that gives us a short term satisfaction (stimulation) at the price of a larger wisdom (love). While American culture seeks to hide from its responsibility in creating much of the world's ills, instead of being the beacon of its salvation, a broader reality will continue to remind who is the true master, whether its through a couple of terrorists with portable A-bombs, or global warming. For they will eventually come, and it definitely grows hotter.

So von Trier shows us there is no escape from this broader reality, or from our human face, that no special effect or big budget will turn us from that mirror, no matter how clever we think we are. We are still, children, really—and just beginning to learn about ourselves. And today, in a world ruled by little boys in suits with dangerous toys, those seeking adulthood need a confident voice. von Trier is such a voice.

THE YIN YANG OF *KILL BILL*

A cultural dialog

by Don Thompson

The omen was clear: I opened the newspaper, and saw two film advertisements facing each other on opposite pages: one for *Kill Bill* and the other
for *Mystic River*. My instincts told me these two films would be an ideal
platform to discuss some ideas that had been percolating in me for a while
regarding what I'll call cultural dialogs—two artists positing alternative
views on what film means and what its potential is within culture.

Also by dialog I mean a kind of collision or dialectic of ideas. When I say
dialectic I mean in the Hegelian (as in the philosopher Hegel) sense: a thesis or idea meets an antithesis or opposing idea, with ideally the result
being the synthesis or new melding of the two that transcends both. In
eastern philosophy the same concept is encapsulated in the form of the
"Yin Yang"—the difference being (in film) that the primary vehicle for the
dialectic is story, while of Yin Yang it is the image. These opposing forces
will come together and merge (often co-opting each other as well as older
forms), and also create cultural choices, forks in the road of history, where
dialog ends and orthodoxy begins.

The core "idea" of Quentin Tarantino's *Kill Bill* is that it questions film form
and cultural conventions in a new and provocative way, while *Mystic River*
is classical in its theme and style—conservative in a sense, and yet fundamentally forward thinking and humanistic. Conversely, Tarantino's film
edges us toward a kind of retro-fascism, even as it goads us beyond humanistic sentimentality to grapple with the essential paradox that anything,
stripped of morality, can become a thing of beauty.

So with Tarantino he uses a cultural fascination with violence, with action,
with the kinetic, as an excuse to play with aesthetic experiments and stylistic meanderings as he gropes for new film forms and new language.
Tarantino apparently believes that greatness lies in finding a way beyond
convention and to define the borders within which culture lives. So he plays
with Godard, he dabbles in Kung-Fu genre and sixties pop culture, he mixes
it all together like a kind of cinematic Emeril, but still, somehow, missing
something—at least in my mind. Tarantino doesn't seem to understand the
idea of the whole, of a final sense of feeling that sums up the piece, the
theme, the idea, what he wants to say—unless what he wants to say
amounts to nothing more than the sum of the stylistic labyrinth he leads us
into. He seems mastered by, not in mastery of, the elements at his com-
mand. He is obviously not a steward of morality, for moral interpretations
are not his responsibility, but ours. Tarantino is the poster child of the fragmented post-modernist, who doesn't believe that any cohesive vision of

truth is possible, and any attempt in that direction would in fact be pretentious. He is the ultimate cynic, who back in ancient Athens would be battling Socrates as he (Tarantino) would try to convince him that there wasn't any cohesive way to "know" anything.

Perhaps what Tarantino "says" is summed up in the end of the film, in the stillness of the snow, and the peace that surrounds the violence of the final scene in the snow-drenched Japanese garden, the Zen like moment of silence that he wants his love of style and his mockery of style and violence to lead us to (it seems). Perhaps what he wants to say is that it (film and the process of making them) all makes him speechless, rapt, and in a state of reverie. But yet there is no movement back from the silence into life—we are only left there hanging, without compass. We are like young children thrown into the pool, and he hopes we swim, and he could care less if we don't. Or better, we are in the labyrinth, with no "golden string" of history and culture strung out behind us to lead us back to sanity and reason.

Some may say if Tarantino tried to tell us where to go or what to feel from there would be tantamount to moralizing—a didacticism that he could never be party to, being that he is fundamentally anti-intellectual in his intellectualism. Tarantino is really the provocateur of a the new outlaw elite, the game boy intellectual who discards all the sham intellectuality and pretensions of enlightened, rational elitism and instead favors a populist Zen that states that God can be found anywhere, even in killing and violence—that God (or in the case of Uma Thurman, the Goddess) is as much lack of compassion as compassion, that the Goddess is as much a killer as a saint.

The limitations of Tarantino lie in the culture as much as himself, the "market" in which Tarantino and most recent film directors seem trapped. The story is really the most basic: revenge. It is single focused and moves forward like a freight train, even if there are a couple of dabblings in non-linear narrative. Tarantino hangs his hat on a thread of a story as an excuse for some kick-ass fight scenes like no other ever filmed—all in services to a young audience hungry to see Uma kick some butt. But these scenes are not so much bloody as beautiful and/or funny, depending on the director's mood. They are also strangely cold, without feeling, yet not without beauty—it is the beauty of ice, of the icy coldness of the stars in a clear night sky. Tarantino's *Kill Bill* is ultimately a comment on nature—that nature is cold, lacking compassion for its inhabitants, and that only the strong will prevail within it. The film, like its American protagonist and country of origin, is aggressive, and the aggression will win out in the global struggle for dominance: the pure White Girl (even if she's called Black Mamba) will defeat the mix-breed Asian whore played by Lucy Liu. Why? Because the White Girl cares more about family than about business, and money is the *raison d'etre* of Lucy Liu's Asian mafioso matron.

The supposed moral (and racial?) purity of Thurman's "Bride"—her "virginity" in her white bride's gown (although she was pregnant at the wedding, an ironic hint at the how The Bride is as compromised as all the others)— her "purity" makes the whole exercise in revenge absurd in the cosmic and existential sense: she battles and kills her foes in the most violent way imaginable to do what? To make a statement, ostensibly, about violence against women, to put a stop to that violence. This is the paradox and absurdity of the warrior, who must fight like hell to protect his/her right not to fight—who is dragged unwillingly into battle, like America into WW II or into the War on Terror. Or at least so goes the myth. Thurman's "bride" is the quintessential American: a loner, a cowboy, an idealist who just wants to be left alone to raise their kids in the vast expanse of the American West (where her wedding takes place)—but those goddamn Asians, half-breeds, flawed one-eyed Blondes, Easterners, and Blacks all are infringing on her God given right just to be left alone.

But the trouble is, she was with them at the beginning: the seed of her opposite was in her from the beginning.

And so it is with the Yin Yang of *Kill Bill*. The Bride is pregnant at her wedding, she is already confirmed to conflict with her innocent myth—she cannot be what she wants to be because she is already corrupted by Bill's seed. The seed of her corruption, like the small white dot in the black half of the Yin Yang symbol (with the White half having the corresponding black dot)— all this means that she will inevitably become her opposite: the mother, protector and giver of life, resurrects again as the assassin. This is the law of Yin Yang and of cultural dialectics—that whatever a thing is, so surely it will become its opposite, just like the day becomes night and each holds within it the seed of the other, the sun and the moon. The Bride, who bears the seed of Bill's child, cannot escape the violence she seeks to flee from.

The gift of philosophy, which is why I bow to it and succumb to it and ultimately try to get readers to love it like I do—the gift of philosophy is awareness. Awareness means growth and growth means avoidance, potentially, of past mistakes. Americans, loath to philosophize because it compromises the ability to act with clarity and conviction (again, so goes the myth), dooms the country to inevitable decline like all other civilizations that came before it. However, there are cracks as we stand on the Razor's Edge of American culture. *Mystic River* is a case in point. While *Kill Bill* revels in violence as art and dehumanizes everything into comic book cliches, and aggressively intimidates us into thinking there is no alternative, it is this gift of philosophy and ability to learn that shows up in a film like *Mystic River*. The film is like the public intellectual who reacts against the futility of post-modernism, egging us on to believe and to embrace the notion of cohesive truths because if we don't we are doomed to the creeping fascism condoned by intellectuals of all stripes who opt out of any kind of social responsibility.

That advertisements for these two films sat on opposite pages of the newspaper said to me in a kind of surreal moment that they were opposing forces in the cultural dialectic, and that Tarantino and Eastwood are participating in a kind of cultural dialog. While *Kill Bill* takes on the cultural and cinematic frontier, and is at the same time courageous and cowardly, *Mystic River*, directed by Clint Eastwood and written by Brian Helgeland (based on a novel by Dennis Lehane), has the surety of a master couched in history, understanding the great lessons of civilization, and not willing to toss them all out in the name of retrograde cultural progress. While *Kill Bill* is like a medieval map of the post modern, with Mexico a bit too big and Alaska much too small, *Mystic River* is an accurate map of the human condition as it sits today. Fundamentally, that condition is tragic, but not without justice at some cosmic level—as if the tragic stories we tell have the potential to redeem us.

Sean Penn's Jimmy is not unlike *Antigone* or *Medea* of the Greek tragedies, a person who because of passion takes matters into their own hands, and with tragic ends. The Greek *namos* or law is personified in detective Sean Devine (Kevin Bacon), who nonetheless comes to understand Jimmy's committing murder as justified on a level outside of the law; because of Dave's (played by Tim Robbins) murder of the child molester, Dave's subsequent murder by Jimmy, if not legally justified, at least brings the tension between Sean and Jimmy to a point of stasis. It is this stasis or balance between individual passion and communal law that is the underlying message of *Mystic River,* and that this stasis or balance happens at a level of a spiritual and human sacrifice that often transcend the laws of the community. *Mystic River* is balanced, cohesive and symmetrical in a way that shows a certain kind of mastery: the mastery of knowing what you want to do and executing on that plan.

It is mastery of intentions, awareness of what the implications of deliberately choosing the mixture of sound and voice and image that makes *Mystic River* such a joy to watch, but yet also makes it safe, like a Rembrandt, as if mastery were frozen in time, and we should accept it and not improve on it—that all of our intellectual meanderings since Plato will eventually bring us back to him. Clint Eastwood has subdued style to story, while *Kill Bill* is all style and no story—a film of form without content, yet exciting and liberating in its dangerous assault on narrative convention. While *Mystic River* bases itself on a book, on the literary traditions of tragedy dating back to Sophocles, *Kill Bill* bases itself on the video game and the Kung Fu movie, with a smattering of Eastern philosophy for good measure (although Tarantino self-consciously forces "chapters" on us, as if to remind us that he knows he's supposed by be literary because he is, after all, an artist).

Marshall McLuhan states that all new mediums, like film, encapsulate older mediums—in the case of film, novels and plays. So video games often encapsulate films or comic books. But with *Kill Bill* there is a devolution: the video game and the comic book dominate—the teenager has taken over the household, tying the geriatric father in the closet, or better, terminating him, like Swarzenegger terminated Gray Davis. Similarly, Bill, emblematic of the corrupt father-patriarch of the polluted mess we've created with globalization, must give way to the pure Aryan woman, Uma, who will destroy him like the old sixties commercial, because "you don't mess with Mother Nature." Or should we say "Mother America"?

While *Mystic River* depends, like the western notion of dialectic, on the unfolding of time and the historical evolution of its story, *Kill Bill* focuses us on the moment and seeks rather to kill time, much like The Bride seeks to kill her male oppressor, Bill. *Mystic River* revels in time, seeing it not so much as an enemy as a sage teacher aching to tell us her secrets and to help us toward reconciliation. While *Kill Bill* has too little story told in too much time, *Mystic River* has too little time for the fullness of it all. In addition, in *Mystic River* nature is to be trusted, rather than dominated and destroyed as in *Kill Bill*—*Mystic River* would have us finally surrender to inevitability of death rather than battle it. In *Mystic River*, any struggle against nature is ultimately futile, as time will prevail and laugh at us: Sean Penn's character of Jimmy cannot find justice or revenge because any justice he seeks, and lack of justice he imparts, can only be seen in the context of his own folly. There can be no heroes in *Mystic River*, no purity and no absolutes within the characters themselves, because all are compromised, and all the living are dead already, and the acceptance of this tragic truth informs the present, makes it somehow sacred. "David died twenty years ago," he says at the end of the film, alluding to the soul death of his friend at the hand of molesters.

The dialectic of *Kill Bill* and *Mystic River* reflects a broader cultural struggle—that is America's razor's edge struggle between the apparent need to aggressively dominate the world and our potential to humanize the world. While our globalistic and imperialistic tendencies currently dominate, as "unwilling" protectors of democracy who must retain vigilance or the Saddams or Osamas will surely destroy us, America walks this fine line, with a tipping point yet to occur that could move the country into total orthodoxy of a kind of corporate, consumer-driven fascism or toward the a humanistic revival that recognizes that Martin Luther King's (among others) message of a human community grounded in tolerance and social and personal responsibility as the only path out of fear and suffering. *Kill Bill* and *Mystic River* are two new films that again express this dialog between America's dark and light sides, America's Yin Yang of conformity and security at all costs, with its handmaidens of corporatism, militarism and technology gone mad, or in opposition, the support of freedom and tolerance, even at the sacrifice of the nation itself. In a sense, Hamilton's pragmatism and Jefferson's idealism are still battling it out, as are the North and the South of the Civil War. If the "pragmatic" cynics and fundamentalists prevail, and they well might, the consumer-fortress of America may well become the nation of the damned, trapped by cycles of violence without escape, perennially reinforcing its myth of freedom even as that freedom has long been legislated out of existence by ever more powerful "Patriot" acts. By then we will have fallen down the path of the Romans, becoming a sham republic under the Caesars — a place even Hamilton and Robert E. Lee would be ashamed of, even as we become fully recognizable to George Orwell as his vision of 1984.

"What links fascism in its various forms is the 'dream of the good community.' The good community based on race, the good community based on religion, the good community based on purity."—Bernard-Heni Levy, author Who Killed Daniel Pearl

THE ELECTRONIC MAESTRO

Vangelis and his legacy

by Timothy Dugdale

In high school, that dismal place to which every teenager is sent to break scholastic rocks in the hot sun, under the watch of men highly reminiscent of Dick Cheney, one had to look hard for fun in the classroom. Ah, but there was Shakespeare. The Bard was a gleeful subversive. Who didn't giggle at the mention of "maidenheads"? I was always partial though to the clock in *Julius Caesar*. It wasn't hard to imagine a couple of old school British hams decked out in togas noting the chimes of an incongruous timepiece. What does it all mean? The anachronism, in Shakespeare's assured hands, served two purposes. On the one hand, it acted as a pre-Brechtian jab across the fourth wall, calling attention to the artifice of the drama. On the other hand, the same punch challenged the audience to consider the relevance of the play to life outside of the theatre.

We don't often think of the anachronism in modern cinema. In a postmodern age, nothing is incongruous. Bogie, resplendent in his tux from Casablanca, can be electronically resurrected and put on a spaceship to Mars and we wouldn't bat an eye. Occasionally, a surprise comes along. For example, Oliver Stone has signed the Greek composer Vangelis to score his next film, *Alexander the Great*. With Stone at the helm, the picture is sure to be a hyperventilating epic, bigger than life, than history itself. So why would Stone commission a score from a man who works almost exclusively with electronic instruments? It does not compute, as it were.

Synthesizers are old hat in Hollywood. They make it easy to sweeten an orchestra while lowering the cost. Thanks to digital sampling technology, anyone can imbue a score with a bit exotica, a gamalan here, a Shakuhashi flute there. Indeed, the synthesizer has thrived precisely because it no longer sounds like a synthesizer. Any of the old trademark sounds of a synthesizer come as standard patches on samplers so. Likewise, new software technology like ProTools, Logic and Garage Band allow composers to cut-and-paste scores from pre-made loops and licks. Everything is in key, nothing is out of time. The machines won't allow it.

In a business as heartless and often headless as the motion picture industry, every artist intent on survival must either find a niche or make one. Vangelis has certainly done that. He has scored other sweeping historical pictures like *The Bounty* (1984) and *1492* (1992) to great effect. So it is perhaps wise to look at the *way* Vangelis composes to understand how he has managed to be such a recognizable presence.

Vangelis Papathanassiou was born in 1943 in Volos, Greece. His earliest musical experience involved doctoring the guts of the family piano. Such adventures might have dissuaded him from more formal study of music. By the age of six, he bade farewell to the music teacher forever. As a teenager, he played in a number of pop bands in Greece, a knock-around existence that culminated in the unlikely stardom of Aphrodite's Child, a trio that specialized in emotional wrought bubblegum. In 1968, the band escaped to Paris from the coup in Greece but they were finished before the decade. Vangelis stayed in Paris where he began to collaborate with the French filmmaker Frederic Rossif.

Rossif was a documentarian who specialized in impressionistic wildlife cine-essays, perfect venues for a multi-instrumentalist anxious to leave pop music behind. Rossif used very sparse narration, often with an elegiac conservationist tone ("Listen well, one day all the animals imprisoned, humiliated, domesticated by man will go far away from us to live once again in the promise of a savage party") leaving plenty of room for Vangelis to experiment. Indeed, the scores for Rossif that have been released on audio disc (*Apocalypse Des Animaux, La Fete Sauvage, L'Opera Sauvage*) attest to the fealty of composer to the philosophical intent of the filmmaker yet also reveal the latitude such non-conventional cinema allowed. The amazing thing about these scores is the speed at which they were composed. One has to return to silent film era to understand Vangelis' unique method. In those days, pianists and organists either improvised on the spot or mined the current hit parade. The talkies killed their business. Movie music was atomized into cues, often afterthoughts to the main production.

Vangelis refuses this model. After screening a film a couple of times, surrounded by his arsenal of keyboards, he improvises a complete soundtrack in one pass. As he can neither read nor write music, the recording tape is his score. By playing "live" to the film, there is little room for egomaniacal impositions on the essence of the film. There is a true and binding dialogue between Vangelis and the frames, manifest in the moment. It is an organic product that breathes on its own in and with the film.

Flush with cash after landing a record deal with RCA, Vangelis purchased an old girl's school in London in 1975 and converted it into his private sound laboratory. And museum. Not only was he an obsessive collector of keyboards, he kept on hand a menagerie of percussive and string instruments. This was long before the advent of the sampler in which sounds could be recorded digitally and then triggered from a keyboard. The whole history of human music was within his reach. And his grasp.

Chariots of Fire

It has been said that Vangelis owes his Oscar to Giorgio Moroder who composed the soundtrack to *Midnight Express*, a winner at the Oscars the year
before. How ironic that *Midnight Express* was conceived and edited using
existing music by Vangelis, pulled at the last minute due to contractual
problems. The same music, I might add, that Carl Sagan used to great
effect in his television series *Cosmos*. Moroder was best known as the pro-
ducer/svengali of Donna Summer. But such a label does him a disservice. On
Summer tracks such as *I Feel Love* and his own Eurodisco epic *From Here to
Eternity*, Moroder injected real sensuality into rhythmic electronic music
that had previously been the domain of German stiffs like Tangerine Dream
and Kraftwerk. His score for *Midnight Express* is rife with that sensuality—
very 70's, very hedonistic, very reckless yet vibrant and feral. The pulse of
the age is in the music.

The score for *Chariots of Fire* was revolutionary precisely because it was
able to speak to the moment yet shuttle us back to 1924. How is this possible? After all, the title theme, with its throbbing bass, clattering percus-
sion, rousing synthetic horns and romantic piano lead has been reduced to
a Hallmark Card that haunts lite FM radio, dentist's offices, wedding
chapels and cancer wards.

But heard inside the film, Vangelis' music is incandescent because it is so
well situated in a larger musical structure. Period music abounds in this
film. Glee club songs, Gilbert and Sullivan ditties and even Parry's towering
ode to Britain, *Jerusalem* appear. This is the music of the England in which
the characters exist—music of churches, fraternities and theatres, institutions constrained and informed by the fading light of Empire and the gentle-
manly delusions of the 19th century laid to rest in the bloody muck of WWI.
Nostalgia is always shadowed by melancholy.

The music of Vangelis belongs to their interior worlds—their ambitions, their
doubts, their convictions. And we see them ennobled by it. Lydell (Ian
Charleson) runs in a race at a country fair held near his Scottish hometown.
The music has the lilt of a local hymn yet also voices Lydell's flailing ecstasy
in competition. Abrahams (Ben Cross) wins the 100 meters in Paris. The race
is shown at regular speed and then is repeated in slow motion accompanied
by the theme music particular to the character. It is little more than a figure, a riff, rendered on a sonorous electric piano. In the background is a
synthesized gull-like sound, reiterating at various rates. Simple, yes. But as

Francis Rimbert, long-time collaborator of French electronic musician Jean Michel Jarre has noted, Vangelis is a mystic—he can play three notes and it's beautiful. In the very next shot, we are in the room of Abraham's trainer barred from the competition because he is a professional. He listens rapturously as the strains of a band striking up the British national anthem reaches his window from across the street. The two sons of immigrants have triumphed, one on the inside looking out, the other on the outside looking in.

The rich deep end of this score is courtesy of live timpani and trap drums, not to mention a titanic Steinway grand. Indeed, it is the acoustic elements of Vangelis' instrumentalism that provide the portal through which the electronics bristle and surge across the years. One does not require suspended disbelief. We never feel the anachronism because it is effectively not there.

At the film's conclusion, when the thundering organ playing "Jerusalem" swells with the choir at Abraham's funeral, it could well be Vangelis at the keys of a cheap toy organ that he has modified to sound epic. We don't know and we don't care. The illusion is complete.

Blade Runner (Director's Cut)

Many critics and academics have hailed this film as an exemplar of post punk or cyber-punk cinema. Yes, the production design of the film exploits a mishmash of visual tropes from Los Angeles 1945, 1982 and 2129. Yes, there's a detective working the margins of a society dominated by technology. I would argue, however, that the score to *Blade Runner* is certainly punk if not in body then spirit. When I think of the Sex Pistols, I imagine that pivotal scene in *2001: A Space Odyssey*, where the ape throws the bone into the air and the match cut reveals a space station, playing in reverse. The Pistols tried to take rock back to the cave. They were reactionaries, moving against the bloated and the banal of the music industry. The synthesizer, once the domain of experimental classical music, was part of the problem. Bands such as Yes and ELP were using it to either fulfill their musical pretenses or to provide sonic filler when pretenses failed them. Their music was horribly white and antiseptic thanks to meticulous musicianship and overproduction.

In contrast, the punks championed filth and noise. Their songs were provisional constructs that could self-destruct at any moment. Knowing how to play an instrument was not only unnecessary; it was unwelcome. Mistakes, bum notes and sundry audio fuck-ups had an air of revolution, a refusal of marketable perfection. Two years before he composed the score for *Chariots of Fire*, Vangelis released *Beaubourg,* a suite inspired by the futuristic architecture of the Parisian edifice. It is a record that detractors call unlistenable because it has no discernable melodies. Yet this is exactly the point. One is forced to engage the work, to go looking inside the abstract expressionism of the sound, to listen actively for the secrets in the noise. Thus, the score for *Blade Runner* is an extension of this sensibility—the imposing yet beautiful netherworld between random noise and music.

The images that capture the essence of Vangelis' score are not in this film. Rather, one must consult the outer and inner sleeve of his 1980 release, *See You Later*. The former features a young reedy Asian woman surveying a bleak washed-out landscape through a pair of futuristic glasses. The latter is even more compelling: a woman carries a child limp in her arms through a greenhouse. They are both wearing gas masks. One is hardly surprised that the centerpiece of the album is a track called *Memories of Green* (perhaps a nod to a fellow trailblazer in electronic experimentation, Brian Eno and his 1975 album, *Another Green World*, which also features a number of somber tone poems). As Vangelis takes a moody and bluesy ramble up and down his beloved Steinway as it is fed through a cheap effects pedal, a studio assistant plays "live" an early version of a Gameboy (That tireless svengali Malcolm McLaren, he of Sex Pistols fame, is in the process of co-opting the second "wave" of punk in what he calls "chip music". Old 8bit Gameboys are now reprogrammed to play music, a reaction against ProTools and the fetish of analogue synthesis in techno). Occasionally, Vangelis dispatches a discreet squall of sample-and-hold white noise. The overall effect is mesmerizing—the music seems at once futuristic and old, as if the composer, like the dazed fugitive in *The Pianist*, happens upon a piano in the midst of post-apocalyptic ruins. Moreover, there is a real tension between harmony and dissonance; neither has the upper hand. The piano appears and then disappears into the ether of beeps and sirens without warning.

By removing both the unconvincing happy ending and the dreary hardboiled narration from the Director's Cut, Ridley Scott did Vangelis a huge service. Imagine what damage would have done to Jerry Goldsmith's dissonant, brooding score for *Chinatown* had Polanski caved into a happy ending? Los Angeles, at any age, is not an uplifting place so why should it sound like it?

Narration gone, Deckard (Harrison Ford) is just another replicant. The film seems less a fiction with protagonists and plot than a documentary about humanoids and the world they're forced to live in by nefarious humans. Vangelis is our emotional guide through the sonic jungle of the film. Every moment, machines and gizmos are chirping, beckoning and inquiring, producing an oppressive din. This of course is part and parcel of the hegemony of the Tyrell Corporation. But Mr. Tyrell is no ordinary tycoon. He enlists a motley crew of anachronistic artisans and craftsman—a broken down Chinaman in a South Pole anorak, a sleazy Middle Eastern bar owner and a dog-eared whiz kid - to do his bidding in genetic design. Everything about their work seems jerry-rigged or fly-by-night, not surprising when you consider their respective laboratories, testaments to the ongoing decay of the city and the lack of first rate manpower.

Thus the most compelling moment of Vangelis' score can be found in the sprawling Dickensian apartment of J.F. Sebastien when Roy appears to tell Pris the bad news that they're down to two. Pris has been softening up the shy J.F. In the background, a cuckoo clock squawks its wisdom. What sounds like a worked over music box begins to play, barely breaking through the chatter of J.F.'s toys. When Roy arrives, the music box melody is lost for a moment as he relates the recent demise of Zora and Leon. Pris replies "Then we're stupid and we'll die." Roy reassures her with a kiss and the music box theme returns, this time richer and more poignant. In this one brief sequence, Vangelis quietly and expertly expresses the existential malaise of these three unfortunate creatures who have little time to live. Circumstances are beyond their control, both inside and outside of their bodies. None of them had a childhood nor will they enjoy golden years dozing in the sun. The music is a wistful elegy, from the toys to them.

The one piece of technology that does not speak until it is spoken to is the piano shipwrecked in Deckard's apartment. Neither Deckard nor Rachel know how to play it. Rachel wonders aloud if she can or if she is merely reproducing the music lessons (a tip of the hat to the old truant Vangelis?) of Tyrell's niece. There is a gallery of antique photographs atop the piano. Relatives of Deckard's or more memory implants? Why this pointless evocation of the 19th century drawing room? The anachronisms of the piano and the photos speak to a world long gone when people had control over noise and their inner thoughts. Memory and imagination could thrive. In that sense, *Memories of Green* is the siren song of ghosts, speaking to an uncertain past. When Deckard takes the Polaroid of Leon's apartment and starts dissecting the thing with the help of a bleeping black box, we see the obliteration of the interior world by the mastery of technology. Nothing is unseen, nothing unknown, no mystery. No memory.

The producer Quincy Jones has noted that black musicians had no interest in the synthesizer until the pitch bend wheel appeared, making experimentation with the "blue note" possible. Nobody knows more about this than Vangelis. The perennial flagship of his arsenal is the Yamaha CS-80, a relic from the late seventies. But at the time of its release, it was the apotheosis of analogue synthesis. Weighing more than 200 lbs., the CS-80 featured a weighted keyboard that mimicked the subtlety of a piano's action. The electronics allowed for the real-time adjustment of many different parameters and effects. Also onboard was a ribbon-controller, which sat just above the keyboard. For Vangelis, this one feature was a godsend, allowing him to flirt with utter sonic chaos one moment, only to slide his finger along the ribbon to release an entirely opposite voicing of rich, melodious strings.

The *Blade Runner* score was a valedictorian moment for the CS-80. By 1982, it was fast becoming a dinosaur. Yamaha failed to follow up on its promise, choosing instead to produce synthesizers that produced sound based on algorithms. From a performance standpoint, this was a disaster. The new machines allowed very little modification of pre-set sounds and what modification was available could only be accomplished by scrolling through time-consuming menus on a tiny LCD screen. The sound was too clean, too bright. Everybody bought the same machines and used the same presets. The synthesizer became little more than a souped-up organ, perfect for new wave and arena rock music of the 80's. Only in the later part of the decade would old synthesizers reappear in the warehouses of Chicago and Detroit where techno was being birthed.

The Legacy

One could say that Vangelis has considerable blood on his hands. The success of *The Chariots of Fire* soundtrack proved that there was money was in the synthesizer outside of rock. Yanni and John Tesh and countless other purveyors of audio anesthesia owe their lives in the New Age and Lifestyle bins of record stores to Vangelis. Indeed, the subdued yet uplifting tone of the *Chariots* soundtrack arrived as just the moment when millions of people needed it: the eighties and the nineties would be a long hard psychic slog and people would need soothing sounds to cope with the va-va-voom of stock market booms and bust.

If *Chariots of Fire* served as the touchstone of one generation's sonic thera-py, *Blade Runner* fit the bill for another. Dozens of chill-out and trance mixes by various DJs (e.g. Paul Oakenfold's *Another World*) use tracks from *Blade Runner* both for atmosphere and gravitas. *Blade Runner*, as men-tioned earlier, is the apotheosis of analog synthesis that carries with it the alluring oppositionality of the film's cyberpunk ethos. It is quintessentially "old school". The shifting, ambiguous categories of the current electronic scene music—ambient techno, downbeat, etc.—reflect the quixotic attempt of youth culture to maintain some sort of taxonomy for itself while staying one step ahead of the music industry. *Blade Runner* stands outside of that system and as such merits reverence.

As Neal Gabler notes in his book, *Life, the Movie*, many people in the developed world have turned to the cinema less for validation of their own experiences than for clues how to live more *like* cinema. Much of current electronic music is really lifestyle music—music for sipping martinis in lounges, music for dancing in clubs, music for chilling at your space age bachelor pad. The overarching yet unspeakable collective imperative is that life is a production that must be scored for potential viewing.

Elvis Mitchell, in his review of *Lost in Translation*, notices signs of a genera-tional affectation of loneliness fetishism. As Charlotte (Scarlett Johanson) admits to Bob (Bill Murray), "I'm stuck". Kevin Shields' score has very little to do with the middle aged travails of Bob. Shield's music is an articulation of Charlotte's momentary dislocation from America and her seemingly more permanent dislocation from her husband and his tolerance of the stupidities of their generation. The self-conscious crosstalk between the melancholic, tonal score and the sound design of the film (the whispered, manicured hush of the hotel, the ringing of phones and fax machines, the incessant clicking of cameras, talking billboards, chiming arcades etc) deeply echoes *Blade Runner*'s moody portrayal of urban hyper-mediation. The future is here, alive and well in Tokyo. And youth have to live with it, much to their mopey chagrin. Indeed, when Charlotte takes a bullet train ride to Kyoto, the sequence is accompanied by the French band Air's *Alone in Kyoto*. The music begins with random electronic noise from which emerges a guitar and a ringing gong-like lead. This is modern life in globalization. The famil-iar and the exotic, noise and music.

But wait, haven't we seen or rather heard this before? Chris Marker's 1982 cine-essay *Sans Soleil* spends a great deal of time exploring Tokyo as a site of "hyperdevelopment". He takes us to temples and arcades and trains, all the while allowing the chaos of Tokyo to fill the soundtrack. Behind that wall of sound is another front of noise, the product of an analogue synthesizer constantly unleashing squalls of random notes and the occasional hint of melody.

In the film, Marker also visits Africa, long considered chronically "underdeveloped." The trickster synthesizer tags along, unflagging in its chirps and gurgles. The central thesis of the film, it seems, is the inconsolable and unbridgeable gap between the first and third worlds. In *Blade Runner*, Vangelis' score articulated the existential quandary of individuals, replicant and human, fighting for breathing room in a corporate world so ruthless and dominating that it had given up on the planet as a human project. The future of man is in space. Earth is left as a graveyard of progress. Marker's film is profoundly melancholic because Japan, caught between feudal heritage and modernist ambitions, races onward into an uncertain and uneasy hybrid of the two. The "climax" of the film involves a vintage stock footage of kamikaze pilots dive-bombing American battle ships. The images have been run through a video synthesizer, rendering the old black-and-white footage vivid red and orange. In the background, one hears Sibelius' *Valse Triste* played by renown Japanese synthesist Isao Tomita. It is as if we were watching a moment of cultural fission during which the old Japan annihilates itself and the modern is born in the primal violence of the explosions. The final image of the film is brief—a hand unplugs the synthesizer (a vintage VCS3) and holds the pin in the air. But what is the gesture? Triumph? Defiance? Or admission of defeat?

This is the true legacy of Vangelis' score for *Blade Runner*. The synthesizer, far from being inhuman and cold, acts as the synapse between incompatible ideas and conditions. Marker, so fixated on memory and history, continues to use the white noise of the analogue synthesizer as trickster, confounding the process of making sense of a world that so often rebuffs these efforts in strange and beautiful ways.

YOUR LIFE IS A MOVIE

Surveillance as culture

by Nicholas Rombes

Today, a second-order reality threatens not to replace the Real, but to expose it as a threat. The final threat. We have been prepared for this by movies like *eXinstenZ* and *The Matrix* and *Minority Report*, which have helped to transform fear into desire. "Big Brother" is no longer a source of anxiety, but of fascination. The Department of Defense's central research arm, the Defense Advanced Research Projects Agency (DARPA) maintains a web site that speaks of "truth maintenance" and "story telling." In an older version of the website, there was this sentence: "Total information aware-ness of transnational threats requires keeping track of individuals and understanding how they fit into models."

What does this have to do with movies? Everything, because movies today are fully engaged with exploring what they have always been about: surveil-lance. Hitchcock's voyeurism has evolved into extensive technologies of looking and tracking and archiving; the very kind of information manage-ment that makes DVDs so popular turns upon a fascination with the cap-tured "in-between" moments of a film: the multiple takes, the discarded lines, the trimmed scenes. If these turn out to be more compelling than the actual movie itself, it is because we are not only tired, but wary of the Real itself that movies tempt us away from. In *Vanilla Sky* and *eXistenZ* and *The Matrix*, characters demand to know the truth because we don't want to. Doesn't some degree of our sadness, at the end of the day, come from our secret recognition that we are parting, more deeply than ever before, with what we used to call the Real?

In *Minority Report*, our futures are monitored from the present, a threat that is strangely exciting on the big screen. We are nostalgic for a world that does not yet quite exist. At last, the world of movies outstrips the real world not by building a better one, but by building a more real one. Citizen-audiences are willing to accept the fact that their lives are no longer private not because they fear terrorism personally, nor because they believe they can purchase their privacy like a commodity, but because they have been prepared for this world by movies, which have accelerated, glamorized, and naturalized these losses of individual freedom and privacy. In this respect, Hollywood has done more than any President or government agency ever could to erase the myth of the private individual.

The loss of privacy—the willingness to let ourselves be monitored—is a form of virtual discipline we are willing to accept, because it is part of the cine-matic logic of voyeurism that is not ubiquitous. Voyeuristic desire is power-ful; it is a desire that great films like Antonioni's *Blow Up* and Coppola's

The Conversation recognize, glamorizing it even as they warn against it. Yet the hazy paranoia of these movies—their inherent distrust of the stories they were telling—has finally proven too difficult today. For all the good and bad things that can be said about the film generation movies of the 1970s, their legacy might very well be that they served as warnings, or at least offered a level of creepy skepticism and paranoia that got audiences thinking about the potentially dangerous ways that the culture was unfolding. The bleak paranoia of George Lucas's *THX 1138* renders it a less watchable movie than, say, *Dark City*, but that's in part because the paranoia, despair, nihilism, and even veiled political critique have become a beautiful commodity. It's not that *Minority Report* is any less subversive than *THX 1138*, but rather that subversion has become a genre in its own right; a relatively safe and marketable category.

The Matrix can raise more wide-ranging, profound, and deeply disturbing issues than any movie of the 1970s, and yet it renders these serious topics too beautifully and glamorously to be shocking. Tom Cruise can worry aloud about government control in *Minority Report*, yet doesn't the movie secretly ask us to admire the vast machinery of surveillance and control, in the same way that *Alien* asked us to admire the creature? Movies like *The Matrix* and *Minority Report* (and even *Spy Kids*) aestheticize power even as their plots declaim against it; they prepare us for the coming Surveillance Culture by making it look beautiful and dangerous in an exotic way.

And there is no escape from their world, because the cinematic vision has triumphed today, tentacled into every facet of popular culture. This may seem like a strange claim to make—have movies ever been separate from pop culture?—but it's important to keep in mind how the divisions among various aspects of popular culture have eroded in recent years. While tie-ins or crossover marketing are nothing new, they have reached unprecedented levels in new media. To take one example: the video game version of *Lord of the Rings: Two Towers*, approximates the film in hyperrealistic ways that positively blur the lines between movie and game. One on-line reviewer, Louise Bedigian, describes the game this way: "Most of the levels begin with a scene taken directly from one of the films. . . . The thing that makes the movie scenes stand out is how they are blended with the real-time polygon game footage. One minute you're watching the actors battle an army of orcs, the next minute you're battling the orcs." Complete with the original music from the film, the actual actors' voices, and the participation of the director, Peter Jackson, the question becomes not "is the movie better than the game?" but rather "do you want to play the movie or watch it?"

The dominant narrative of our society is cinematic: educators talk about how to make their classes more visual; the White House renders war cinematic (or at least videomatic); video games refashion and sometimes literally inject cinema into their games; cell phones play movies; flash animation and Quicktime renders the internet increasingly more fluid and motion-like. Cinema has spectacularly colonized nearly every pop cultural, political, and social space. Even academia—with its tradition of dissent and critique—is saturated with the cinematic vision. At M.I.T.'s Program in Comparative Media Studies, for example, there is a new project called "Games to Teach," (http://web.mit.edu/cms/News/newmodels.html) described this way: "As part as Microsoft i-Campus, a five-year research alliance between MIT and Microsoft intends to explore best practices in game design and production and current educational theory." The description of the program goes on to say, "Henry Jenkins [Director of Comparative Media Studies] and his colleagues believe computer and video games are emerging as a powerful new teaching medium that enables robust interactivity, providing for new pedagogical models." Jenkins says that "The challenge of the Games-to-Teach Project will be to create science and engineering content in a compelling narrative form that students want to engage with."

The risk in saying this, I know, is that it sounds defensive, conservative, maybe even Luddite. For who can deny the pure visual joy of our cinematic landscape, the triumph of the camera eye? It was the dream of the modernists, after all. Films like Vertov's *Man with a Movie Camera*, or Weine's *Cabinet of Dr. Caligari*, or Varda's *Cleo from 5 to 7*, all projected a kind of jump-cut, cinematic state of mind, a life based on motion and shifting perspectives. It seems that this should be a good thing: cinema always has the potential to smash and rearrange the old ways of seeing. Its perpetual assault on reality always comes with the potential for radical change.

Like the characters in David Cronenberg's *eXistenZ*, we find that we have been in the game all along. "Real life" is merely a staging point for deeper and deeper penetrations into the fake world that has become, in fact, our real one. The sweeping victory of cinematic vision—from pop culture to education to politics—is only the latest and most dangerous stage of our evolution out of the old reality and into the new. The promise of movies—ranging from *Metropolis* to *Blade Runner*, from *Fight Club* to *Mulholland Drive*—has always been that they gave us the imaginative spaces to test out the alternate worlds they were projecting. But they always depended on the counterpoint of the real world as a basis for comparison, a kind of constant against their variables.

Don't think you are spared. For your life, too, is a movie, a soundtrack for someone. You have been documented. Whose home movies are you in? Who watches you in your car at the intersection? Who has recorded your voice, saved your e-mails, archived your purchases? For someone, you are a prediction waiting to happen. You have been prepared for this all your life, watching movies in the dark, spying. The Orwellian future you learned to dismiss is here, and now you are waiting—eagerly perhaps—to see the fangs.

Contributor and Interview Bios

Eric Alterman

Eric Alterman is professor of English at Brooklyn College of the City University of New York, media columnist for *The Nation*, the "Altercation" weblogger for MSNBC.com, and a senior fellow at the Center for American Progress, where he writes and edits the "Think Again" column. Alterman is the author of numerous national bestsellers, including *What Liberal Media? The Truth About Bias and the News* (2003,2004), and *The Book on Bush: How George W. (Mis)leads America* (with Mark Green, 2004). His newest book is *When Presidents Lie: A History of Deception and its Consequences*, (September, 2004). His *Sound & Fury: The Making of the Punditocracy* (1992, 2000), won the 1992 George Orwell Award and *his It Ain't No Sin to be Glad You're Alive: The Promise of Bruce Springsteen* (1999, 2001), won the 1999 Stephen Crane Literary Award.

Ray Carney

Ray Carney is a professor of film and American studies at Boston University where he was, for the past decade, director of Film Studies and graduate admissions. He is the author of numerous books on American and European art film, including: *The Films of Mike Leigh: Embracing the World; Speaking the Language of Desire: The Films of Carl Dreyer; American Vision: The Films of Frank Capra; Why Art Matters; Necessary Experiences*; and *What's Wrong with Film Criticism ... and Everything Else*. He is also the world's leading authority on the life and work of John Cassavetes and has published many books on the filmmaker: *The Films of John Cassavetes: Pragmatism, Modernism, and the Movies; American Dreaming: The Films of John Cassavetes and the American Experience; Cassavetes on Cassavetes; John Cassavetes: The Adventure of Insecurity*; and the BFI monograph on *Cassavetes' Shadows*. His two-volume intellectual biography of the filmmaker is scheduled for publication in 2006. Prof. Carney is also a scholarly authority on 19th-and 20th-century American painting, literature, drama, music, and philosophy. He contributed essays on pragmatist aesthetics to Morris Dickstein's *The Revival of Pragmatism: New Essays on Social Thought, Law, and Culture* and Townsend Ludington's *A Modern Mosaic: Art and Modernism in the United States*, co-curated the Beat Culture and the New America show for the Whitney Museum of American Art, and contributed extensively to the catalogue. He is a popular speaker at events around the world and manages a web site devoted to film and other art at: *www.Cassavetes.com*.

Patricia Ducey

Patricia Ducey writes fiction, essays, and screenplays from her home base in California. Her screenplays and teleplays have placed in the top rounds of the Nichol and Austin competitions, and her flash fiction and essays can be found at several e-zines, such as *the-phone-book, Vestal Review,* and *Mississippi Review*. She earned an MA in Critical Studies (film) from Chapman University and wrote her thesis on Irish film after happily researching the subject in Galway, Dublin and London.

Timothy Dugdale

Timothy Dugdale teaches in the Department of English at University of Detroit Mercy. He is also the founder of *Atomic Quill Media*, and is the author of two crime fiction novels published through Black Moss Press.

Shelley Friedman

Shelley Friedman studied under Ray Carney at Boston University and received her Bachelor of Science in film *magna cum laude* in 2000. Since then, she has worked in New York City as a film editor, associate producer in documentary television, contributing writer for *MovieMaker Magazine* and *SolPix*, and as an independent filmmaker. She currently lives in Los Angeles.

Todd Gitlin

Todd Gitlin is a nationally known authority on the media and society. His articles have appeared in many publications including *The New York Times, Newsday, Los Angeles Times, Dissent, Observer* (London), and *The Chicago Tribune*. His books include: *The Sixties: Years of Hope, Days of Rage; Inside Prime Time; The Twilight of Common Dreams: Why America is Wracked by Culture Wars*; and the prize-winning novel, *Sacrifice*. His latest book is

Media Unlimited: How the Torrent of Images and Sounds Overwhelms Our Lives. He is the North American editor of *opendemocracy* and a member of the editorial boards of *Dissent, The American Scholar,* and the *Journal of Human Rights.* He is also a professor in NYU's Culture and Communication and Sociology departments.

T.B. Meek

T.B. (Tom) Meek is a contributing film critic for the *Boston Phoenix* and member of the Boston Society of Film Critics. He ramblings and rants have also appeared in *the Fort Worth Star-Telegram, Film Threat* and *E! Online.* He lives in Cambridge, Massachusetts, practices yoga religiously and rides his bike everywhere. Tom is currently working on a collection of short stories that take place in Boston and the surrounding cityscape.

Kayoko Mitsumatsu

Kayoko Mitsumatsu has written, directed, and produced dozens of feature documentary programs for NHK, Japan's National Public Broadcaster. Her programs include *First They Killed My Father* (based on the bestselling book from Harpercollins, about a Cambodian survivor of the Pol Pot regime), International Emmy-nominated *Jyakuchu: Magical Artist of Edo*; *Stolen Vermeers*; *Child Abuse*; *Class Action Against Petrochemical Corporations* – to name a few. Currently she is working on documentaries about Alzheimers, TIVO and (for the world market) *Lost Islands of the World and the Women Who Speak for Them,* and *Betrayed by the Rising Sun: The Comfort Women of the Imperial Army during World War II.* She currently lives in the United States.

Michael Neff

Michael Neff is the creator and chief editor of *WebdelSol.Com.* He is also Executive Director of the WDS Association, and a publisher of several literary arts magazines including *Del Sol Review, 5_Trope, In Posse Review, Perihelion,* and *La Petite Zine.* His own literary work has appeared in numerous publications including *American Way* (First Annual Faux Faulkner Contest*)*, *North American Review, Pittsburgh Quarterly, Quarterly West, Conjunctions, Octavo,* and *The Literary Review.*

Rob Nilsson

Rob Nilsson is an internationally-acclaimed director working as a film artist for over 20 years. He is the first American director to have won both the Camera d'Or at Cannes and the Grand Prize at Sundance (*Heat and Sunlight, Northern Lights*). His film *Chalk* was the 2nd film to be streamed in its entirety over the Internet and was released theatrically in 2000. His film *Attitude* opened theatrically in New York City in 2003. Rob continues to be one of the most influential voices in digital cinema, and is considered a pioneer in the field who has consistently demonstrated innovation and integrity. You can learn more about Rob at his website *www.robnilsson.com*.

Nicholas Rombes

Nicholas Rombes is a professor of English at the University of Detroit Mercy, where he teaches courses in film, creative writing, and literature, and where he co-founded the Electronic Critique program. His books include *Ramones* (Continuum) and *New Punk Cinema*, which he edited. His essays and other work have appeared in *Ctheory, Post Script, Arizona Quarterly, Exquisite Corpose,* and *McSweeney's Internet Tendency*.

Mike Shen

Mike Shen was an early contributor to SolPix, and his essays and reviews for focused on "the film and fiction fusion" — the intellectual and artistic territory where film and fiction converge. Mike currently lives in California.

Don Thompson

Don Thompson is a filmmaker, playwright and essayist. As a playwright, he was known through the 1980's and 90's for his plays *Tibet Does Not Exist* and *L.A. Book Of The Dead*, as well as for his more recent *Democracy: A Work In Progress* (2004-2005). His first feature film, *Clouds,* received awards and special recognition at six film festivals, also garnering a theatrical distribution deal with IN Pictures in 2000 and was later released on DVD in 2004. In 2001, he co-founded (with Diana Takata) nextPix, a production company based in New York City, and is currently developing and producing documentary and narrative feature films.

DEL SOL PRESS, based out of Washington, D.C., publishes exemplary and edgy fiction, poetry, and nonfiction (mostly contemporary, with the occasional reprint). Founded in 2002, the press sponsors two annual competitions:

THE DEL SOL PRESS POETRY PRIZE is a yearly book-length competition with a January deadline for an unpublished book of poems.

THE ROBERT OLEN BUTLER FICTION PRIZE is awarded for the best short story, published or unpublished. The deadline is in November of each year.

http://webdelsol.com/DelSolPress